MAO TSE-T

MAKERS OF MODERN THOUGHT

EDITOR:

MAO TSE-TUNG

by

JACK GRAY

Secretary of the Chinese Studies
Committee of the
University of Glasgow

LUTTERWORTH PRESS
GUILDFORD AND LONDON

First published 1973

by the Lutterworth Press, Luke House, Guildford, Surrey

American edition published by the Judson Press, Valley Forge,
Pennsylvania

ISBN 0 7188 1899 7

Printed in Great Britain
at the St Ann's Press, Park Road, Altrincham, Cheshire
WA14 5QQ

CONTENTS

1

THE RISE TO POWER

ON MAY THE FOURTH, 1919, the students of Peking University burst into the streets of the capital to protest against the failure of the peacemakers of Versailles to support China against Japanese pressure, and against the venality of the republican government in Peking towards Japan's demands. The movement they began, as they harangued the Peking population, with their toothbrushes in their pockets and their towels over their shoulders, ready to go to gaol, swept China. It drew the support of students and intellectuals, of the new Chinese middle classes, and of the workers in the cities of China. The movement failed in its immediate political aims, but it started a landslide. For the first time all classes of urban China (the peasants were yet to be roused) had united in defence of the nation, foreshadowing the possibility of democratic nationalism. For the first time, the younger intellectuals of China repudiated Confucianism and turned their hopes to 'science and democracy'. The Nationalist Party, the already old-fashioned leadership of the revolution, were swamped in this nationwide ferment which was both an opportunity and a danger to them. The old literary language was rapidly replaced by the colloquial style of the despised popular literature, so that the young radicals could reach a far wider audience, as a first step to democratic education. An irreversible psychological change took place, a 'cultural revolution'.

On August 18, 1966, the students of Peking once more poured into the streets, this time to attack those who, they believed, had betrayed the revolution, to drown the official revolutionary party in a torrent of new ideas, new activities, and new organizations, to demand a system of education which would make a reality of democratic participation and equality of opportunity, and to destroy the still vital remains of conservative social and moral attitudes which stood in the way of continued change. They launched a new 'cultural revolution'—this time by name—whose avowed purpose was to produce an irreversible psychological change.

The link between 1919 and 1966 was Mao Tse-tung. Seventy-three years old in 1966, he could remember leaving Peking in 1919 to hurry back to his home province of Hunan to spread the student movement there, to organize student strikes, to publish a radical student newspaper, to throw himself into an attempt to create a system of mass education with the students as its backbone. His own passionate faith in revolution from below, in the essential nationalist solidarity of the mass of the Chinese people, and in the vital role of the young in the processes of change, stems from May Fourth. The world looked with alarm on the rampaging school-children of 1966; but Mao Tse-tung had seen them and been with them in action before, at what had proved, through their efforts, a turning point in Chinese history. Under his guidance, under the inspiration of his own 'da-zi-bao' poster on the walls of Peking University, they may well have turned the course of Chinese history once more.

Early Life

Mao Tse-tung in 1919 was 26, a new graduate of a teachers' training college. His father was a peasant who, from poverty, had raised himself to the position of the most prosperous peasant in his village in Hunan province. Mao Tse-tung, like so many of his generation, rebelled against his father's authority, an authority made harsher by his successful but grinding struggle to give his family security. Clearly he came to stand in Mao's mind for the type of the successful individual peasant in a poor society, forced into a mean and narrow poverty of spirit by insecurity and pre-carious dependence on his own family's labour on their tiny patrimony—disciplinarian, suspicious of education, anti-social, ready to exploit ruthlessly those just a little poorer than himself, with no vision beyond the diurnal struggle with the soil. Mao's own vision of society is a reaction against these demoralizing constraints; and Maoism is as concerned with moral as with political and economic liberation.

Mao had been born into a world in which all the old values had been shattered. It was scarcely possible to begin to diagnose China's ills in detail, in the absence of shared new aspirations and possibilities by which analysis could be directed.

Three-quarters of a century had already passed since China had been dragged into the modern world by her defeat in the Opium War and the Treaty of Nanking in 1842, which forced the Chinese to accept the European international system, and laid her open to the colonial ambitions of the Western powers and Japan.

The Opium War had been a shocking experience. China was undisputed master of the Far Eastern world, combining with herself, Manchuria, Mongolia, Turkestan, and Tibet in a single state, fringed with tributary nations in Korea, Annam, Burma, and Nepal. Proud of her civilizing mission in which her Confucian philosophy, her written language and its literature, her law and her arts had been accepted by the surrounding peoples, China had been able to sustain the myth that her Confucian system represented the supreme achievement of human moral potentialities, and that civilized government existed only in the Chinese emperor and his Confucian-trained servants. Eight thousand British and Indian troops, disposing of a fire power beyond the dreams of Chinese soldiers, shattered the defences of this Empire, and forced the Emperor to humiliating concessions. When the Chinese sought to evade the Treaty, Britain, accompanied by France, made war on her again in 1857 and this time took the capital.

Meanwhile, the discredit of the Manchu government opened the rift, by then all but healed, between the Chinese and their Manchu rulers. Internal rebellion on a vast scale plunged province after province into chaos and destruction.

The provinces, forced to take care of themselves, took over the powers of the central government, weakened its control of the country, weakened even its ability to deal with the foreigners who now treated as freely with provincial viceroys as with the imperial government, and reduced the bankrupt ruling house in Peking into humiliating dependence upon foreign money and support. Disaster was heaped on disaster. Burma, Tibet, Korea, Annam, Mongolia, Taiwan, and much of Turkestan were drawn out of China's control. In 1904 Russians and Japanese fought over Manchuria as if China did not exist. In the Treaty Ports, foreign enclaves which the Chinese had been forced to concede to the powers, the Chinese were humiliated almost as much by good advice as by supercilious behaviour.

China's Internal Problems

Foreign power, however, only complicated the historic internal problems of the country. Of these, the chief was the problem of land tenure. The operative ideal of Chinese society had been the belief that every family should own enough land for its own support, should own no more, and should owe nothing to anyone except the light taxes paid to the state in return for protection against invasion, disorder, flood, and drought. In practice this peasant ideal was perhaps better upheld in China than in most other countries. Nevertheless, throughout Chinese history there had been something of a cyclical movement in which peasant proprietorship broke down in the face of all the misfortunes which could assail peasant families working on a narrow margin above subsistence, and then was restored, usually by successful revolt. The peasant rebellion of the Taipings in 1850 and the peasant movements of the 1920s were nothing new.

What was new was that China's population had begun to increase at an unprecedented rate from the seventeenth century onwards. The traditional man-land ratio was totally changed. Increased land hunger sharpened the tenancy issue, while the mere redistribution of land in the traditional way would no longer relieve poverty. A revolution in production was now necessary, even to sustain the old standard of life.

Foreign trade complicated this situation, at least locally, by the destruction of peasant handicrafts by foreign competition and by machine competition from foreign-owned factories built in China's cities, depriving many peasants of the auxiliary occupations by which they had eked out the inadequate income from their farms. On balance, Western economic operations probably stimulated the Chinese economy, but local competition could produce local situations of great distress and great political significance.

The Chinese were slow to react. The first generation of officials who were forced into regular contact with the foreigners listened to their arguments about the inexhaustible benefits of a free development of industry and trade, and rejected them. The price would have been the destruction of Confucian society, based on the settled farming family and its morality, and stressing the frugal use of resources. The mandarins were fearful of the social disruption which experience of even China's existing and very carefully limited mining and urban industry already demonstrated, and fearful of the loss of prestige and power which the Confucian élite would suffer in a world dominated by entrepreneurs and experts instead of by an élite trained in the moral norms of Confucianism. This generation were willing to imitate foreign arms and foreign military drill in order to oppose the foreigners; beyond that they wanted no industrialization, and no change.

Modern arms, however, were not effective in the hands of pre-modern soldiers. Change had to go further. Meanwhile a handful of Chinese, influenced by the growing availability of translations from Western books, and by the slow creation in the Treaty Ports outside Chinese jurisdiction of a new and partly Westernized middle class, began to appreciate that foreign strength was not based upon gunboats, but on a way of life which embraced legal, political, social, and economic conditions. The disastrous defeat in 1895 of China's new army and navy by the Japanese touched off an attempt in China in 1898 to create a constitutional monarchy, and through this to abolish the traditional Confucian examinations, the sinecures, and the traditional élite itself, and replace

11

them by a political system designed to encourage economic growth and the creation of national strength in conscious imitation of Japan. This attempt at peaceful reform failed; the vested interests in the old system were still overwhelmingly powerful.

Beyond China, however, among the communities of emigrant Chinese in South-East Asia and California, who had accepted a far greater degree of Westernization and who were outside (although not entirely free from) the pressures of Chinese society, a revolutionary movement was growing up, led by the son of an emigrant family in Hawaii, Sun Yat-sen. On October 10, 1911, the tenth of Sun's risings in China, now backed by Chinese secret societies which had been founded three hundred years before to oppose the Manchus, succeeded. Sun's secret-society adherents in the imperial armies forced the Emperor to abdicate, and a Republic was created in 1912.

Civil War

This change, drastic as it might appear, changed little in practice. Power passed into the hands of the greatest of China's new military leaders, Yuan Shih-k'ai; and the newly created Chinese parliament was reduced to impotence and disgrace by intimidation and corruption. Sun's revolutionary party was driven into South China, to survive on the favours of local military commanders. On Yuan's death in 1916, China broke up among his provincial commanders and plunged into twenty years of civil war. The new warlords with their half-armed, half-starved, and half-paid armies lived off the country like locusts, destroying across much of China the normal fabric of social life. Powerful local interests, old and new, grouped themselves behind the provincial warlords, the more so as signs of unrest among the poor, made desperate by chronic civil war, began to increase. Protest and repression then fed each other in an escalation now only too familiar.

Public spirit and social conscience were overwhelmed in the devastation of civil war. The Chinese did not take kindly to this. They are a moral people. Perhaps no political system can fully express the moral aspirations of a community except an advanced democracy, in which the community can bind itself to moral obligations through legislation freely accepted and fully obeyed. The Chinese had never had this; their morality as a community had therefore never been fully expressed at a national level; but with all qualifications made, they represented the greatest moral tradition outside Christendom, and its collapse in the twentieth century was deeply felt. The Chinese were humiliated to observe that the detested foreign tyrants so often practiced better what the Chinese still so piously preached, and frequently showed more charity to the Chinese than the Chinese themselves.

But what to put in the place of the old morality, dependent upon a moral authority now totally discredited by the very fact of the substitution of a republic for the monarchy?

New Ideas

Youth, very properly and predictably, felt these moral problems more intensely than their elders. It was among youth that the new ferment of ideas began when Mao Tse-tung was a student in his early twenties. It is important to appreciate the materials on which these young minds were working. Their scope was by no means narrow. They included their own vast heritage there to be re-interpreted; the main classics of Western European literature; the records of the Japanese experience of modernization; and by 1919 some acquaintance with the various socialist traditions—social democracy, the paternalistic 'socialism' of Bismarck's Germany, anarchism, and finally Marxism-Leninism. Mao Tse-tung's early reading can illustrate this scope.

Although he is not a classical scholar and would not claim to be, Mao had read a great deal in the Chinese classics, as well as the range of classical texts which were the basis of a traditional education and which he frequently quoted. His most influential teacher, Yang Ch'ang-chi, was a classical scholar who had spent a decade abroad, and who sought to find common ground between Western and Chinese intellectual traditions. Mao received from him an education which stressed the seventeenth-century nationalist thinkers of China and brought their ideas into relation with those of Kant and T. H. Green. To this Mao added a knowledge of the traditional vernacular novels which were as widely read by Chinese children as they were roundly condemned by their educated elders; these novels all represented in varying degrees a revolt against the orthodox mores, and the most famous of them, *The Water Margin*, was a glorification of rebellion, China's Robin Hood legend.

During the erratic and self-willed course of young Mao's search for an education, his reactions to this desultory reading and experience (expressed in articles written for the radical journals of the time) show already both the general lines of thought of his generation, and his own idiosyncratic reactions. By 1919 the chief writings of Montesquieu, Adam Smith, Rousseau, J. S. Mill, Darwin, and Spenser were available in Chinese translation. Part of the *Communist Manifesto* had been translated, and Engel's *Socialism Utopian and Scientific*. Kautsky's ideas were available, and also a then influential history of socialism by Kirkupp. In philosophy, Kant, Hegel, and T. H. Green were being read and discussed, and Paulsen's *System of Ethics* was very popular. Young Chinese could not on this basis gain a critical and detailed knowledge of Western thought, but at the same time almost every major trend in European and American intellectual development was represented in translation. The political and moral choices made by Mao and his generation were not made in ignorance of alternatives.

Each, however, reacted in his individual way. Mao in particular was an eclectic; although he became a Marxist, he did not therefore find all other systems of thought to be without value. His attitude was marked by three characteristic divergences from the Marxist norm.

First, his interest in pragmatism was expressed in his founding of the 'Society for the Study of Problems' in which he insisted on empirical study of actual situations as a basis for theoretical generalization; 'isms and problems' was the pragmatist Hu Shih's phrase contrasting the ideological with the practical, and the title of Mao's little study group points directly and sympathetically to Hu Shih's pragmatist emphasis.

With the collapse of the power of the landlords, the peasant associations have now become the sole organs of authority . . . All decisions are made by a joint council consisting of the magistrate and the representatives of the revolutionary mass organizations . . . The adoption of a democratic committee system of government should not therefore present much of a problem in Hunan . . . In a few months the peasants have accomplished what Dr. Sun Yat-sen wanted, but failed, to accomplish in the forty years he devoted to the national revolution.

In a famous passage, Mao summed up the political potential of this movement:

In a very short time, in China's central, southern, and northern provinces, several hundred peasants will rise like a mighty storm, like a hurricane, a force so swift and violent that no power, however great, will be able to hold it back. They will smash all the trammels that bind them and rush forward along the road to liberation. They will sweep all the imperialists, warlords, corrupt officials, local tyrants, and evil gentry into their graves. Every revolutionary party and every revolutionary comrade will be put to the test, to be accepted or rejected as they decide. There are three alternatives. To march at their head and lead them? To trail behind them, gesticulating and criticizing? Or to stand in their way and oppose them? Every Chinese is free to choose, but events will force you to make the choice quickly.

Scholars have tended to concentrate on the question whether Mao's emphasis on peasant revolutionary potentialities, as opposed to the potentialities of the urban working class, was heretical; but what is perhaps more important is the faith which he shows in the capacity of the peasants not only to seize power, but to use it when they have won it. There is a very great contrast between Mao's acceptance of the possibilities of spontaneous organization and Lenin's fear of spontaneity.

This acceptance marked a new stage in the development of Chinese radical thought. All Chinese radicals, Nationalist and socialist alike, appreciated that China's élitist traditions offered the greatest single obstacle to successful radical action.

All agreed that they must create a leadership 'trusted by the masses'. Only Mao, however, out of his experience in Hunan, took the final and necessary step from this to the idea of a leadership which *would trust the masses*. Out of his argument against those who feared peasant anarchy came a characteristic of Maoist thought which has been a major premise ever since: that the masses, even the most deprived and down-trodden, can be trusted to rise to the responsibilities of power.

Throughout the report, Mao insisted that the seizure of political power was fundamental:

> Once the peasants have their organization, the first thing they do is to smash the political power and prestige of the landlord class . . . This . . . is the pivotal struggle . . . Without victory in this struggle, no victory is possible in the economic struggle to reduce rent and interest, to secure land and other means of production, and so on . . . The political authority of the landlords is the backbone of all the other systems of authority. With that overturned, the clan authority, the religious authority, and the authority of the husband all begin to totter . . . No one any longer dares to practise the cruel corporal and capital punishments that used to be inflicted in the ancestral temples . . . In many places the peasant associations have taken over the temples of the gods as their offices. Everywhere they advocate the appropriation of temple property in order to start schools and to defray the expenses of the associations . . . As to the authority of the husband, this has always been weaker among the poor peasants because, out of economic necessity, their womenfolk have had to do more manual labour . . . The women in many places have now begun to organize rural women's associations.

Everything followed, therefore, from the seizure of political authority: not only the possibility of economic changes, but immediate spontaneous movement toward cultural and social change, including the immediate imposition of a frugal and puritanical morality (which Mao has ever since assumed to be a proper expression of poor-peasant dominance) and a burning interest in education. The seizure of power by the armed masses, exercising their initiative through omni-competent Paris-Commune-type committees of government, has remained central to Maoist thought. It is only when the masses have seized power that their aspirations are fully revealed; therefore it is only after the seizure of power (on however local a scale) that the mass-line process of leadership can operate fully. The seizure and exercise of power form the critical first step in the process of education.

In spite of Mao's advice, the Communists discouraged the Hunan peasant movement in an attempt to preserve the united front with the Nationalists. Chiang K'ai-shek, the Kuomintang leader, having taken Shanghai on April 12, 1927, could now kick away the prop of Soviet help and depend upon the support of Shanghai business; he broke with the left wing and slaughtered hundreds of his former Communist associates, in spite of their efforts to avoid provoking him. Too late, the Communist Party sought the peasants as allies. Mao was sent back to Hunan to try to rekindle the embers of the fire of peasant revolt which the Party had first lighted and then trampled out. It proved a hopeless task. Mao's forces retreated south to the mountainous borders of Hunan and Kiangsi, and in the Chingkang mountain range set up a rural Soviet.

In an important sense, the die was cast. Not only had Chiang's *coup d'état* polarized Chinese politics into two armed extremes and rendered the social-democratic middle helpless and impotent, but in a deeper sense also the future of Chinese political development was now determined as a choice between two very different roads to revolution. All Chinese radicals had agreed that change in China must take place village by village, where the real social and political power lay, and that democracy must be built from the grass roots up. Neither Nationalists nor Communists had achieved much in this respect, although the left wing had done more than the right. However, Chiang K'ai-shek feared Communist influence in the local Party branches and the mass organizations. He was embarrassed also by their vociferous demand for the unilateral abrogation of the unequal treaties. Chiang crushed his grass-roots organizations, and so left himself with no alternative but to try to impose revolution from above. The attempt was futile. Reforming legislation could not be enforced in the villages without a democratic movement there to inforce it. The new elected institutions at village level proved totally ineffective, because the rich, through their clan connections and their close ties with the local officials, were able easily to maintain and even extend their power by assuming control of the new institutions.

Rural Revolution

The Communists, on the other hand, in the face of successive 'extermination campaigns' by Chiang's armies, came to depend more and more on the existence of Mao's territorial base in the mountains. The survival of this tiny state within the state became their primary consideration. As guerrillas, they could operate only among a friendly population; so ideology had to give way to policies which could command the support of the vast majority of the villages of their area. The Communists began a long and painful apprenticeship in the government of the Chinese village, an apprenticeship which was to last for twenty years and to rid them of the urban bias and the contempt towards 'the idiocy of rural life' which prevailed in other Communist parties. They were committed to a rural grass-roots revolution.

Their agrarian policies during the six years' existence of the Kiangsi Soviet provide the best illustration of the changes they underwent. During the alliance with the Nationalists, the Chinese Communists, being dependent on armies officered largely by the sons of landlords, could not afford to advocate a thorough redistribution of land. After Chiang's coup, however, they swung to the opposite pole, and the first land legislation of the new Soviet was of an extreme kind. All land was to be confiscated and redistributed in equal allotments per head. But the existing Chinese village was by no means completely polarized into a rich minority and a landless majority. On the contrary, like Chinese society as a whole, it was 'big in the middle and small at both ends'. The division into poor, middle, and rich peasants was artificial as applied to China. By every index of class position—land-ownership, debt, or income—Chinese village conditions presented a

22

smooth curve from poor to rich. Moreover, although these three classes differed in size, as far as they could be distinguished, each made as a class an equal contribution to the marketed surplus of agriculture.

It was impossible in China, unlike parts at least of Russia, to solve the land problem by an egalitarian redistribution, because thirty to forty per cent of the population would have lost by it; it was also impossible, as in Russia, to control the marketed surplus by dispossessing a small rural élite who produced almost all of it. On the other hand, the complexity of the Chinese village gave ample opportunity, by the use of flexible policies over rents, debts, and taxes, to gain a substantial majority for each policy. Within a year, the process of compromise had begun and, with many halts and twists, by 1933 had reached the point (advocated by Mao Tse-tung himself in 1927) where land reform mainly took the simple shape of abolishing tenure, with only marginal changes in the operation of farming as opposed to the ownership of land. Where probably most farmers were at least part tenants, this was more palatable. The price was that the poor, though now less poor, were still not on terms of equality with the more prosperous. But this compromise of 1933 was the basis of the final Agrarian Reform Law of 1950.

Mao's part in this has been misunderstood. Because he insisted that there must be virtually a second redistribution of land (since the first, undertaken when the rural élite still had power and prestige, could not hope to be fully effective) it has been suggested that he took a leftist view of land reform. The evidence is to the contrary. Mao's reports from the Soviet, coupled with the texts of the successive land programmes, show his readiness to sacrifice ideology to the economic and political viability of his territory.

The first years of the Kiangsi Soviet had a sobering effect in other respects. If the Hunan peasant revolt showed the revolutionary ardour of Chinese peasants at its height, the Kiangsi Soviet showed it at its minimum. It was uphill work in this backward and mountainous area. The clan system was powerful and cut across attempts to create class consciousness. The native inhabitants were at loggerheads with recent (by Chinese standards) immigrants, and when the under-privileged immigrants sided with the Communists, the natives automatically took the other side, so that the Party became an instrument in communal strife. The poor and backward inhabitants of the area were too cowed by their rulers to respond to the offer of representative government and democratic participation: they left the Party in unwanted whole and sole control of the new organs of government. Mao was emphatic that people must be induced to take part in decisions affecting their own lives, but the problem remained; and the ease with which Chinese, even if they were Communist Party members, slid readily back into bureaucratic attitudes could do little to improve the situation.

Throughout its existence, the Kiangsi Soviet was under military attack. In the first years there were serious disagreements over military policy. One group in the Party wanted to fight campaigns purely guerrilla in nature, sweeping the widest possible areas to propagate Communist ideas. Mao opposed this; no support for revolution would be forthcoming from people who knew that the Red Army would soon move on and leave them to the revenge of the Whites. Mao advocated the cautious gradual extension of the frontiers of the Soviet, with military and political consolidation behind. On the other hand, he also opposed making a fetish of the retention of territory, and insisted that the immediate purpose of war was not to hold territory but to destroy enemy forces; and that, outnumbered and out-gunned as the Red Army was, and dependent as it was on the support of an armed and committed militia, the best tactic was to draw the enemy deep into Communist territory where his disadvantages were at a maximum. Mao and Chu Teh (Mao's military commander and founder of the Red Army) evolved a system in which the small Communist forces, strong in their loyalty and willing to undertake forced marches of great length and rapidity, used this simple but effective form of superior mobility to concentrate superior forces against one section of the enemy at a time. In this way, Chiang K'ai-shek's four 'extermination campaigns' were successively defeated. By the time of the fifth, however, the very success of the Chinese Communists' little Soviet tempted its leaders to try to defend its frontiers. It was defeated, the Soviet was evacuated, and the Long March began.

The Red Army moved westward, with no fixed idea of its destination. The arguments and manoeuvres within the Party were complicated. Suffice it to say that in the end Mao Tse-tung advocated moving north to Shensi, in order to form an anti-Japanese alliance with the troops of Chang Hsueh-liang whom the Japanese had driven out of Manchuria, and with Yen Hsi-shan, the warlord of Shansi, whose territories were likely to be the next object of Japanese attention. This policy won the day. The Communist Party was aware (and worried) that Shensi would be a poor base from a social point of view. as there was little tenancy and therefore little revolutionary potential. To compensate, they might win the opportunity of fighting the Japanese.

Leader of the Chinese Communist Party

It was in these circumstances that Mao Tse-tung finally and formally became the leader of the Party; and the issue on which he won is not without significance: as a patriot, he marched towards the Japanese, though towards that part of China which offered the least prospect of social revolution.

The gamble came off, though it was costly. Only a small fraction of the Kiangsi forces reached the Yellow River after melodramatic privations in a march of 4,000 miles. But the Manchurian troops refused to obey Chiang K'ai-shek's orders to wipe out the sick and hungry remnants of Mao's forces. When Chiang came north to Sian to enforce his orders, he was kidnapped and forced to agree to a United Front against the national enemy. The following year, 1937, the Japanese began their attempt to conquer North China.

The Communist administration relinquished their more radical policies, such as land reform, for the duration. Instead, Mao's government set out to hoist the Nationalists with their own petard. Chiang retreated before the Japanese, 'buying space to gain time' until America should enter the war; the Communists (with no greater stomach for decisive battles) advanced, though mainly by guerrilla operations. The Nationalists had not been able to enforce their own law reducing land rents by 25%; the Communists enforced it. The Nationalists had been unable to reform the gross inequities of the land tax; the Communists maintained their government and their war effort until the crisis of 1942 without taxing more than a minority of proprietors, and thereafter provided an equable system of progressive taxation. The Nationalists had tried and failed to establish democratic local government; the Communists established it. The Nationalist leaders called for sacrifices and lived in luxury themselves; the Communist leaders created a legend of patriotic austerity. In 1936, the Communists had been forced to plead for Chiang's life from his angry captors because even as Communists they recognized that no other leader could rally the Chinese against the Japanese invaders; by 1945, Chiang was widely regarded as a traitor and a reactionary, and every educated adolescent in China had secretly read Mao's *New Democracy*.

Meanwhile, Maoism had come of age between 1942 and 1944, typically out of swift and practical reaction to an emergency. P'eng Te-huai (purged in 1959 for his conventional opposition to Maoist mass-line economic and military policies) in 1940 launched a conventional attack on the Japanese, the Hundred Regiments Offensive. It was successful, but it called down upon the victors a retaliation which they could not resist by conventional military means. The Border Regions were reduced in size until their population was halved. At the same time, the Nationalist government withdrew its subsidies to the Communist administration. The situation was desperate. The means of war had to be maintained, and increased, from a population reduced by half and living at the poor subsistence level of the millet-eating regions of the Northwest.

Mao's policy was to dismantle the administrative apparatus of the Border Region, to send its personnel down to the villages to lead a vast co-operative production campaign, and to insist that all administrative, military, and educational institutions should grow their own food and cotton in order to become as nearly self-supporting as possible. He insisted

26

that it was impossible to tax the peasants of the region, except out of increased production and increased personal incomes—'this is the only possible basis of protracted war'.

The political problems of this drastic reorganization were great. The dispersed personnel of the central government would not take kindly to the loss of authority and prestige. Mainly young city intellectuals attracted to Yenan by the legend of Communist patriotism, they often knew little of Chinese rural life and tended to despise the illiterate peasant leaders in the villages, who in return resented the interlopers. Members of administrative and professional institutions were reluctant to take to the physical labour necessary for self-sufficiency. Those Party leaders who had absorbed Russian ideas of war and of administration opposed the break-up of the administrative machine.

The problems could be summed up as follows. First, it was essential to create an effective local leadership able to learn local conditions quickly, able to gain the confidence of the peasants, and able to take independent action. Second, and as a corollary, it was necessary to create a unifying ideology firm enough to support such independent action. Mao's theory of leadership, his philosophical theory of knowledge, with its supporting theories of art and literature, and the first adumbration of his strategy of economic growth, grew out of this crisis which succeeded the Hundred Regiments Offensive.

Mao's arguments with his colleagues over the internal policies of the Border Regions were accompanied by a running polemic with the Kuomintang, in which he sought to assert the leading role of the Communist Party in China's future. His *New Democracy* provided a blue-print for a coalition government led by the Communist Party but including representatives of all parties of the left and centre, including the left wing of the Kuomintang.

At the end of the war against Japan, Mao further elaborated his ideas in *On Coalition Government*. The title was significant. The American government was strenuously attempting to persuade Nationalists and Communists to join in a coalition in order to forestall and prevent civil war. It was probably a hopeless task from the beginning; the Communist

Party would not wholly relinquish their separate territorial and military existence, their only guarantees of personal as well as political survival; Chiang would accept nothing significantly less than their total surrender. The Soviet Union was as anxious as the United States to maintain the Nationalists in power and gave only sporadic and insignificant support to Mao Tse-tung. The guns soon began to go off by themselves, and full-scale civil war had developed by 1947.

Military and Political Victory

The Communist Party prepared for five years of heavy fighting, but Nationalist resistance quickly collapsed. The repressiveness of Chiang's government offended most politically conscious Chinese. No one any longer expected radical reform from it. Hyperinflation destroyed what little credit it had left. The Nationalist troops voted with their feet, joining the Communist-led forces. The Communists' military victory obscured the political victory which was truly decisive; the coalition government they offered was the more convincing.

On October 1, 1949, Mao Tse-tung said 'The Chinese people have stood up'. It was the message that most Chinese wanted to hear. The nation was whole again. The defeats and the humiliations were over. Corruption was over. Self-disgust was over. To most Chinese, the victory of the austere and sober young volunteers from the North-west, with the red star on their caps, represented moral rebirth; and the symbol of this moral rebirth was the peasant school teacher who stood high above the crowd on the Tien-an Men Rostrum, the focus of an impassioned new national loyalty founded in a re-awakened social conscience.

Mao's Family

Little is known of Mao Tse-tung's personal life. This is true of most Communist leaders. The convention is that the home life of the leader is irrelevant. In some respects, indeed, we know more—or at least we know some more interesting things—about Mao's early life than we do about the lives of some other Communist leaders, because of his autobiographical reminiscences to Edgar Snow. These reminiscences, however, are full of the wisdom of hindsight and coloured by Mao's own later political development. One cannot take Mao's account of his own childhood and youth too literally. Too much of the writing on Mao is either scurrilous or hagiographic, and too much of it is full of speculation about the possible influence of Mao's early personal relations on the formation of his character and therefore on the formation of his political attitudes. Such speculation is pointless, because we simply do not know enough about Mao's early life to permit depth psychology analysis; it is ludicrous even to attempt such a thing. Moreover, many of the characteristics which have been distinguished as personal to Mao, and explained by the circumstances of his early life, such as his hostility to his father and his rebellion against parental authority, were common to most of his generation, and do not reflect any individual characteristic.

In the case of Mao Tse-tung, his near-total absorption in politics and in thought about politics perhaps represents the most important truth about him, but one which by its nature precludes any detailed knowledge of his character. Moreover, we only have Mao's word for this rebellion.

Perhaps the most remarkable thing about Mao's character is the fact that he has been able on the whole to maintain an attitude of generosity to defeated enemies, has carefully limited bloodshed, and has almost totally eliminated revenge, after a life which has been personally tragic and in which most of the tragic bereavements were brought about by the executioners of the Nationalist Party.

Those closest to Mao in his own generation in his family were associated with him from their earliest youth in revolutionary agitation and organization. His brother, Mao Tse-min, played an active part along with Mao Tse-tung in the establishment of workers' organizations in the early 1920's, and then became a student in the Institute of the Peasant Revolution in 1925. He occupied a prominent position in the Kiangsi Soviet as a financial and economic expert, his fortunes rising and falling within the Party with those of Mao

Tse-tung. He took part in the Long March and then was sent to Sinkiang as financial adviser to the warlord Sheng Shih-tsai, who at that time found it expedient to favour the Communist Party. When Sheng transferred his allegiance to the Kuomintang, Mao Tse-min was imprisoned and shot.

Mao's other brother, Tse-tan, had a similar career. Eight years younger than Mao Tse-tung, he was educated at the primary school attached to Changsha Teachers' College, where Mao Tse-tung himself was a student. He was with Mao in the Autumn Harvest uprising of 1927. Thereafter, he worked underground in Hunan, and was prominent in the organization of land reform in the Kiangsi Soviet. When the Soviet was evacuated, he was caught and executed. Tse-chien, Mao's adopted sister, was also closely associated with his early revolutionary efforts. She too was executed, in Hengyang in 1929.

In 1920, Mao married Yang K'ai-hui, the daughter of his teacher, Yang Ch'ang-chi. K'ai-hui was already taking a full part in political agitation before her marriage, and she joined the Communist Party in 1922. She bore Mao two sons. Trained as a journalist, she was active in education and in mass organization through self-education movements. She was working underground in Changsha when Mao Tse-tung and Chu Teh attacked the city reluctantly, in obedience to the Central Committee's orders. After the retreat, K'ai-hui was caught in the city and executed.

Mao Tse-tung in 1931 married Ho Tse-t'ien, the politically active daughter of peasants whom he met in Kiangsi. They were divorced in unknown circumstances in 1938, and some months later Mao married Chiang Ch'ing, a left-wing actress and film star who had come to Yenan in 1937, and who played a prominent part in the formation of revolutionary drama during the Border Region period. She remained associated with propaganda drama thereafter. In 1964, she headed the reform of Peking opera, and in 1966 she became a member of the Cultural Revolution Group in Peking, with a special responsibility for further reform of the drama and the film.

Of Mao's two sons by Yang K'ai-hui, one was killed in

30

the Korean War in 1950. The other apparently survives. The two children of his marriage with Ho Tse-t'ien were left behind in the care of peasants when the Kiangsi Soviet was evacuated, and never found again.

Mao's personal history is thus a story of the loss by enemy action of most of those he held dear. Those who deplore his aphorism, 'Political power grows out of the barrel of a gun', should remember this background, and remember that when Mao talks about 'steeled in struggle' he knows what he is talking about.

2

POLITICAL AND ECONOMIC THOUGHT

THERE is a general opinion in the West that Mao Tse-tung is an impractical idealist cut off from reality, that his political philosophy puts questions of ideological purity above those of practicality, that he believes that moral exhortation can replace material and personal incentives in the development of socialism, and that he believes that the human will can overcome the constraints of reality.

It is a strange indictment of a man who once wrote, 'There is no "ism" in the world which transcends utilitarianism.'

How is this paradox to be resolved? Perhaps one should begin by stating what would be generally agreed and that is that Mao, in his earlier years, was the most pragmatic and practical of Marxists. It may be, however, that in his old age he has lost touch with reality. This is the question that has to be answered.

The 'Mass Line'

Let us start with the concept which Mao Tse-tung himself, and all his commentators, hostile or sympathetic, would agree was the centre of his political thinking and of his political style: the 'mass line'. Its essence is expressed in a single paragraph in his essay of June, 1943, on *Some Questions of Leadership:*

> In all the practical work of our Party, all correct leadership is necessarily 'from the masses to the masses'. This means: take the ideas of the masses (scattered and unsystematic ideas) and concentrate them (through study, turn them into concentrated and systematic ideas), then go to the masses and pro-

pagate and explain these ideas until the masses embrace them as their own, hold fast to them and translate them into action, and test the correctness of these ideas in such action, then once again concentrate ideas from the masses and once again go to the masses so that the ideas are persevered in and carried through. And so on, over and over again in an endless spiral, with the ideas becoming more correct, more vital and richer each time. Such is the Marxist theory of knowledge.

We will discuss the elaboration and the application of this idea in different circumstances at a later stage. For the present, it is enough to note that whatever this method of political leadership may mean, it certainly does not suggest the dogmatic imposition from above of *a priori* ideas determined by ideology. The vital sentence is the last one: 'Such is the Marxist theory of knowledge.' Mass-line politics are an application of the Marxist theory of knowledge. They represent in Mao's mind the policy application of the proper relationship between theory and practice. This point is made clear by the fact that in the paragraph elsewhere in which Mao sums up his theory of knowledge, the parallelism between the two passages is very striking. In his philosophical essay *On Practice,* Mao states:

Discover the truth through practice and again through practice verify the truth. Start from perceptual knowledge and actively develop it into rational knowledge. Then start from rational knowledge and actively guide revolutionary practice to change both the subjective and the objective world. Practice, knowledge, again practice, and again knowledge, this form repeats itself in endless cycles and with each cycle the content of knowledge and practice rises to a higher level. Such is the whole of the dialectical materialist theory of knowledge and such is the dialectical materialist theory of the unity of knowing and doing.

The theory of political leadership which is implicit in these two passages has its historical roots in Chinese society, in Chinese cultural attitudes, and in the conditions in which the Chinese Communist Party had been forced to work since the Party was driven from the cities in 1927. It refers to ideas, situations, and problems of which all twentieth-century Chinese radicals were fully aware and with which they were concerned.

First of all, China is vast and varied, and its physical and social circumstances were scarcely known in detail even to the Chinese Communists themselves. Mao complained that the Chinese middle classes had proved incapable of the effort necessary to study Chinese conditions, and that the Chinese Communists themselves must make the effort. In the preface and postscript to his *Rural Surveys,* he put forward in simple practical terms the methods by which investigation of local conditions could best be carried on. His advice in *Rural Surveys* represents his theory of knowledge at is simplest, and it is on such simplicities that the Maoist theory of knowledge is based.

Traditional Chinese political attitudes and behaviour and expectations were admirably designed to maintain stability and keep the peace in a society where change was slow and imperceptible and was regarded with suspicion when recognized; but they presented a serious obstacle to any attempts at radical change. All Chinese radicals, Communist and Nationalist alike, accepted the idea that the central problem of the Chinese revolution was to create a new kind of political leadership capable of winning the support of the mass of the people for the rapid and continuous changes necessary in Chinese society. As far as the need for a truly popular leadership is concerned, the very words of Mao, which so many Western commentators assume to be personal to Mao himself, were the current, though frequently debased, coin of political discussion in China throughout the early twentieth century. The need for a new leadership, trusted by the mass of the people and responsive to popular demands, was the starting point of the idea of the mass line.

Communist experience from 1927 reinforced the mass-line idea. Indeed, the very physical survival of the Communist leadership and its active followers in the Kiangsi Soviet period as guerrilla soldiers, depended upon majority support in widely varying local circumstances. Something akin to mass-line methods was therefore dictated from the start. The failures of these years could be interpreted in such a way as to show that the neglect of the mass-line always ended in political defeat, first in the Hunan peasant movement, second in the disarming of the Shanghai workers in 1927, third in the refusal to ally with the Fukien rebels, fourth in the early doctrinaire attempts at land reform in the Kiangsi Soviet, and finally in the disastrous attempt at a conventional defence of the Kiangsi Soviet in the Fifth Encirclement Campaign.

The anti-Japanese war demanded an appeal to the widest possible cross-section of the Chinese population, and this situation gave the mass-line idea a new and nationalist dimension. Then in 1942 came the crisis which succeeded the Hundred Regiments Offensive, dictating the dismantling of the top-heavy state administration and the use of its personnel to maximize the resources of the reduced border areas by leading co-operative production campaigns.

Thus when the Chinese Communist Party came to power in 1949, many of its members, including Mao, believed that a majority of the Chinese population would support radical change; that the means of winning this support was to provide a leadership which arrived at its policies through the articulation and rationalization of mass demands; that for this purpose it is the quality of local leadership which is vital; that in a situation in which the masses are step by step led to a clearer view of their interests until they accept more and more radical action, the processs of political recruitment must involve the constant shedding of leaders who have fallen behind in consciousness and their replacement by new more radical types; that traditional élitist attitudes, the traditional distaste for conflict, and the traditional quasi-family patron-client relationships of Chinese society were obstacles to effective radical action; that these could be overcome only by a mass-line style; and that leadership, if it is to be based upon popular aspirations in varying local conditions, must be a process of mutual education of leaders and led, expressed in a theory of knowledge which stresses the acquisition and interpretation of knowledge as a continuous and dynamic process in which both leaders and masses are involved. It came to be accepted that, provided the conditions implied above were met, continuous progress indefinitely prolonged could be expected through creative conflict. This creative conflict would be maintained by differences of interest and opinion within a popular consensus, and would yield a process of accelerating political consciousness and effective action.

The implications of some of these points are worth pursuing a little further. The belief that radical action could win the support of a majority of the population has come to be enshrined in Mao's insistence in a variety of different political circumstances that 95% of the Chinese population could be brought to accept Communist policies, and it is to be noted that this statement, essentially descriptive, has been used in many political campaigns with prescriptive force: if 95% of the population cannot be won to support Communist policies, then these policies have not been carried into action in a proper and effective manner. To Mao, politics is a process of radicalization because it is a process of rationalization. A rational view of any social situation is bound to show the need for change, or for further change, and a proper dialectial view of any situation even if that situation represents a triumph, will reveal new things to be done. The result of the solution of any problem is another problem, though at a new and higher level of achievement. The more recent slogan, 'Divide one into two', has this as one of its implications.

The process of arriving at policies through the articulation and rationalization of mass demands is similarly continuous and never-ending. Moreover, through the trial implementation of policies thus derived, and through their correction and improvement, or their replacement as a consequence of mass criticism, a process of education through participation is involved. The masses learn the value of new ideas, new institutions, and new social forms through practice under mass-line leadership, and every success should lead to new aspirations and to an increase in the rationality with which the masses face their problems.

The implication for the importance of local leadership is that effective mass-line methods must be to a large extent decentralized methods.

36

The idea that in the process of radicalization the first natural leaders who emerge are likely to be superseded is one of vital importance in Maoist politics. Its implication is that no leader has a prescriptive right to continue in power. The leaders can keep their place only by continuing to lead.

In the Cultural Revolution, this was applied to the entire Communist Party, which was virtually destroyed and then rebuilt by revolutionary committees in which the politically active among the non-Party population participated in the choice of new members of the Party or in the promotion of existing members. What applies to individuals also applies to institutions. In the crisis of the Border Regions, when the central government was dismantled, Mao put forward emphatically the idea that institutions exist only for practical purposes, and that if they cease to perform a useful function, and *a fortiori* if they become obstacles to necessary change, then they must ruthlessly be dissolved and replaced.

Mao's Approach to Obstacles

Mao's ideas of political organization and behaviour were further elaborated in this context in dealing with the obstacles which China's traditional political culture presented to effective modern political action. It is important in examining these aspects of Mao's ideas to look on them first and foremost as attempts to provide a practical solution for practical problems, even although the solutions may be expressed in abstract theoretical terms. If they are approached in this way, it is then possible to determine how far, if at all, the theory goes beyond the practical necessities of the case to become ideological.

The most fundamental problem of Chinese traditional political culture was the élitist assumptions which Chinese, when they were given authority, inherited from the national past. The old imperial élite had, in theory, totalitarian power. As the representatives of the emperor's quasi-paternal moral authority, they could intervene in any aspect of life. Organized opposition to their authority was impossible; they could be petitioned but they could not be replaced by popular will. Their task was not to accept the existence of sectional interests and reconcile them, but to prevent such sectional interests from ever achieving political organization and political expression. They were an intellectual élite; and moreover the Confucianist examinations which they had to pass were a test, not of practical skills, or even of intellectual skills, but of moral knowledge, essentially a test of the 'internalization' of the orthodox values of Chinese society. Finally, a thousand years of malpractices had made of the Chinese mandarinate an élite as distinguished by a sense of its own privileges as by its sense of responsibility. And as a privileged class they had in traditional China no rivals; the only path to power was through officialdom. It is no wonder that popular attitudes towards the mandarins (applied inevitably to their modern successors in both the Nationalist and Communist parties) were ambivalent, perhaps accepting on the one hand their moral right to rule, but detesting the whole class with few exceptions as careerists, so that the vast majority of Chinese positively avoided contact with officialdom.

This was the situation with which all radical leaders in twentieth-century China had to deal. The leaders of the Nationalist Party had found no means to deal with this élitist tradition except by futile moral exhortations. Mao sought the cure in another direction through the mass-line process of mutual education of leaders and led, through his insistence that to the maximum practical extent all cadres would share the life of the people, their living conditions and their physical labour, and through real and effective equality of opportunity in education.

Of almost equal importance was the distaste for conflict which was part of Chinese psychology, expressing itself, on the one hand, in the world's most developed sense of good manners, but, on the other, in the inability to conceive of the possibility of limited and creative conflict. This distaste for conflict could lead to false unanimity, unprincipled compromise, the postponement of decisions, the refusal to criticize others openly or to accept criticism oneself, and, in the last resort, to open and destructive conflict among irreconcilable cliques. In a word, the lack of appreciation of the possibilities of creative conflict made normal committee consultation and committee government extremely difficult. This was a fundamental problem of political organization in China. Rules had to be laid down for political conflict within the Party. This Mao Tse-tung sought to do, mainly in the course of the Rectification Campaign of 1942-44. The slogan 'Unity-criticism-unity' was used to sum up these rules. It is a slogan which was already familiar in the Communist world before Mao Tse-tung used it, but while in Soviet Russia the stress is on unity, in China the stress is on criticism.

It has been widely assumed in the West that the purpose of 'Unity-criticism-unity' was to secure uniformity, but its implications are the opposite. Its purpose is to make effective discussion and effective representation of different views possible. Moreover, it does not end with renewed unity, which by Maoist definition is only provisional. The result of renewed unity would normally be experimental application of policy. Renewed discussion and criticism is then bound to follow; and the process is endless. The best means of dealing with the Chinese tendency to turn every relationship, even political relationships, into a personalized patron-client connection which results in heirarchy, is of course the effective co-operation of equals in committee consultation. But the tendency to think in heirarchical terms, the reluctance to co-operate with equals, the dependence on the authority of superiors, and the 'commandist' attitude to inferiors, still inevitably persist in China and must still be faced.

Mao's theory of knowledge is partly a response to the bookish and authoritarian nature of traditional Chinese education, which is another important factor in Chinese political attitudes. This lies behind his undoubted bias towards pragmatism. This is not obvious from the more philosophical statements which he has made about the problems of achieving knowledge and of making judgments. Here he has naturally been determined to be an orthodox Marxist. It is the context of his statements, the history behind them, and their practical application in policy which make Mao's restatement of these Marxist points of interest and significance.

Mao's fundamental problem in the Border Region period was simple. The leadership of the Party was being recruited from two contrasting sources: on the one hand, from peasant guerrillas, and, on the other, from young urban intellectuals who had crossed China to join the Communists' Anti-Japanese Movement. Their attitudes were worlds apart.

The intellectuals knew something of China as a nation, of the world beyond China, and of the long-term perspectives of change. They suffered, however, from the élitist notions of the Chinese educated class and from the impractical nature of Chinese education. Much of the authoritarianism of the traditional education system had been carried over into modern educational institutions, limiting the ability of the educated to form their own independent judgments. It gave no incentive whatever to intellectuals to study with industry and sympathy the problems of the peasant in gaining his livelihood, and led them grossly to underestimate the intelligence and knowledge of China's peasants, who operated a system of agriculture which, though it did not use modern inputs, was far from primitive or simple, and was indeed by far the world's most productive pre-modern form of agriculture.

The village peasant leaders, on the other hand, while knowing their own local conditions intimately, and appreciating local problems from their own experience, could not be expected so readily to understand the national situation or the world situation or the long-term future.

Somehow, these two streams of recruitment had to flow together effectively to produce cadres who had the strong points of both, who shared common aspirations, and who could work together without jealousy and misunderstanding. For this reason, it is often possible in Mao's writings almost to replace 'theory' and 'practice' with 'intellectuals' and 'peasants'.

The Communist Party's situation in the Border Regions, fighting a guerrilla war against the Japanese from scattered base areas and guerrilla zones, left much of the Party's practical operations in the hands of local leaders, dependent mostly upon local initiative, and largely outside any effective administrative control from the centre. It was necessary to attempt to create unity in variety so that shared aspirations could guide autonomous local policy. The relation between theory and practice which Mao suggested was thus meant to contribute to the solution of this problem of the co-ordination of guerrilla war. In some of the arguments therefore, 'theory' and 'practice' could well be replaced by 'the border region as a whole' and 'the individual regions and guerrilla zones'.

There was yet another dimension to the argument. Mao's rivals, especially during the early Border Region period, were a group of relatively young Communist leaders trained in Moscow and much less familiar than Mao and his group with the actual conditions of China. In this context, theory and practice represent Marxist-Leninist generalizations based on European and Soviet experience on the one hand, and on the other the necessity of modifying these generalizations to fit the very different circumstances of China. In this way, the argument over theory and practice became involved with the 'sinification' of Marxism.

In this situation, whatever the balance between theory and practice might be in the mind of Mao Tse-tung, the problem was, generally speaking, one of 'theory' carried to excess, and Mao is therefore emphatic that in the circumstances of the time the deviation towards dogmatism rather than the deviation towards excessive empiricism was what had to be fought. He was forced indeed to defend himself against the charge of excessive empiricism. But the simplicity of the instructions which Mao Tse-tung felt called upon to give on the necessity of studying real conditions, and his constant reiteration of these simple points, would in itself be evidence of the magnitude of the problem with which he had to deal.

In the development of Mao's theory of knowledge we have seen the working out of his determination to transcend the contradiction between Marxism and pragmatism, the two great protagonists of the chief intellectual controversy of his youth; and although he is the most pragmatic of Marxists, yet he is no less a Marxist. To Mao, analysis and investigation of conditions means analysis and investigation in Marxist terms of class interest and class conflict. Mao Tse-tung has never fallen into the vulgar Marxism of regarding a man's character as being entirely predictable on the basis of his class origin. Yet he has never doubted that, at least as a matter of statistical probability, class interests will determine social and political attitudes.

But no Marxist has been more concerned than Mao with the idea that members of an exploiting class are themselves the victims of that alienation from reality which their class position forces upon them; and he brings to this problem a characteristic Chinese belief in the infinite possibilities of education, and through education of a successful change of heart in the individual landlord or member of the borgeoisie. In China, of course, the sharing of anti-imperialist feelings by all classes has been a powerful solvent of class prejudice. The necessity of operating in a social situation where there were few clear boundaries of class, and the opportunities of a political situation in which class conflict could for the time being be overcome by national solidarity, induced Mao to take a much subtler view of the operation of social contradictions. They did not however make him any less convinced of their reality or of their primacy in determining the political configuration of China. Nor is he any less a nationalist for being a Marxist.

The Theory of Contradictions

In many ways indeed Mao Tse-tung puts Marxist dialectics to more serious use than any Marxist since Lenin. The rise to power of the Chinese Communists was a protracted process in constantly changing political circumstances and vastly varied geographical and social conditions. To analyse these circumstances in a way consistent with Marxist beliefs, Mao was forced to elaborate at considerable length on the idea of contradiction. In doing so he perhaps stretches the word 'contradiction' to cover so many kinds of conflict, opposition, dichotomy, and dualism that the world is deprived of any definable and philosophical meaning. The consistency and the value of Mao's arguments concerning the 'principal contradiction' and the 'principal aspect of the principal contradiction' can be left to experts in dialectics. In practical terms, the theory provided a rule of thumb by which to arrange, in a coherent relationship, the relations of the Chinese Communists with the various groups within the Nationalist Party and their supporters in the country, the puppet Kuomintang government in East China, the Japanese invaders, and the Western powers. It also gave a rule of thumb by which hard-pressed local leaders could resolve problems of priority among the manifold tasks which they had to carry out.

Whatever the merits of this elaboration of the idea of contradiction, there are two suppositions which Mao Tse-tung has derived from his use of dialectical analysis, which are striking parts of his philosophy. The first is that conflict is an inevitable part of society, even of classless society. Even when antagonistic class conflicts have disappeared, sources of conflict will still be found in the differences of opinion which different types and levels of experience produce in different groups and classes of people, the more so as knowledge can never be complete, and the truth as known at any one time is only relative and subject to more or less dispute. Mao clearly goes further than this. He regards such conflict as healthy, and fears lest it should be smothered. If conflict were smothered, then that would be the end of social progress, because conflict is the fuel of social progress and the motive power of politics.

The second point of dialectical philosophy which Mao has constantly emphasized, perhaps not explicitly but in the nature of his policies and opinions, is that contradictions must be transcended, not simply compromised. Thus his theory of knowledge is not a simple compromise between Marxism and pragmatism but an attempt to make Marxism more effective by making its operation fully pragmatic, and to make pragmatic action more effective by giving it a Marxist orientation. In the same way, in his struggles with the problem of central control versus local initiative, he has not sought compromise, but some new view of the situation which would produce at

43

once more effective central direction and more effective local initiative. The communes represent the synthesis of this contradiction.

Before further analysis of Mao's political ideas, we may turn to his economic ideas and policies as the most clear and striking application of his theory of knowledge and mass-line style. It is in the economic context that Mao has been most strongly attacked for his lack of realism and his imposition of ideological and doctrinaire considerations. An examination of his economic ideas and policies, therefore, may be the best way to make his real position clear.

Economic Ideas

The evolution of Maoist economic ideas began, like so much else in Maoism, in the experience of the Border Regions after 1942. The use of co-operative enterprise as the basis of labour-intensive land reclamation and irrigation, in the attempt to develop the resources of the Border Regions quickly, provided the germs of two important Maoist ideas. The first was the possibility that advance to the full collectivization of agriculture could be gradual, beginning with the simple forms of co-operation represented by the war-time mutual-aid teams. The second was the idea that the economy of rural China could be developed and transformed through a process which would begin with the full use, in co-operative forms, of surplus labour, which would move through a period of the use of simple intermediate technology, paid for by the profits of the initial investments of labour, and would end with the diversification and industrialization of the country-side and the full mechanization of agriculture.

These two ideas, of course, are not separated in Mao's mind. Co-operation among the local community is necessary to ensure the achievement of the minimum scale of organization for the effective use of surplus labour. Co-operative accounting is necessary to ensure that the members of the community are pledged to save and to invest a part of the proceeds of their efforts at construction.

These ideas were the basis of the collectivization of Chinese

44

agriculture between 1951 and 1956. During the period of the First Five Year Plan, 1953–57, the Chinese economy was planned and organized on the Soviet model as far as industry was concerned. Rural policy, however, was an exception to the general prevalence in China of Russian ideas. Here, these Border Region precedents were dominant. This, however, was the result of a struggle within the Chinese Communist Party. The failures of Soviet and East European collectivized agriculture were well known to the Chinese, and throughout the Communist world there was disillusionment with the idea, or at least with the current practice, of collectivized farming. In China, there was, in addition, an argument against collectivization at that time which did not exist with the same force anywhere else in the Communist world. One of the main points of socialist organization of agriculture was to create farms large enough for the economic use of modern machinery.

In China, however, where at least 20% of the farming population was under-employed, there seemed little point in attempting to mechanize agriculture unless and until the State was in a position to provide alternative employment in modern industry; and it was obvious that the State would be unable to do this in China for many years, perhaps generations, to come. It could therefore be argued that there was little point in China in the collectivization of agriculture until its mechanization became desirable. Moreover, industry in China was far too under-developed to provide the means of agricultural mechanization, even if it had been economically rational.

Mao and his supporters, however, insisted that in Chinese conditions 'institutional change must precede technical change'—in other words, that the co-operative organization of agriculture was a necessary precondition of successful mechanization, and not an institutional consequence of the completion of mechanization. We now know from documents made public during the Cultural Revolution that K'ang Sheng visited the Soviet Union in 1953 to investigate Soviet collective agriculture and had returned to China very critical indeed of Soviet policy. He believed that investment in mechanization in the Soviet Union had not paid off in higher production and he stigmatized the Soviet tractor stations, which at that time were the primary means of providing machines to the Russian collectives, as 'mere tax collecting stations' which 'blackmailed the peasant'. The controversies over the relevance of mechanized agriculture and over the form which mechanization should take, and over the question of who should pay for it, who should control it, and how long the process of mechanization should take, played a key part in the arguments within the Party over the speed-up of collectivization in late 1955, the Great Leap Forward in 1958, and the Cultural Revolution.

With this key controversy in mind, let us look briefly at the economic strategy which Mao Tse-tung proposed to use in relation to the gradual collectivization of Chinese agriculture. This strategy is expressed in the preface and comments by Mao interspersed throughout *The High Tide of Socialism in the Chinese Countryside,* a collection of descriptions of Chinese co-operative farms published at the very end of 1955 to justify the speed-up of the collectivization movement which Mao Tse-tung then advocated successfully.

The most famous of all the co-operatives decribed in this collection is the one identified with its leader, Wang Kuo-fan. It was a dramatic *a fortiori* case of how to break out of the poverty trap by the use of surplus labour. Wang Kuo-fan was a member of a mutual-aid team. He and the poorer members of the team decided that the time had come to form a proper co-operative. The more prosperous peasants involved in the mutual aid team, however, would not join it, and without their savings and tools there seemed very little prospect of forming a successful co-operative. Wang Kuo-fan insisted that it was still possible, provided its poor members were able to find some means of raising the money for the small investments necessary in simple tools.

He pursuaded his fellow-members of the new co-operative to spend the winter in the hills collecting fuel for sale in the towns. For this they needed no equipment except bill-hooks and carrying-poles. By normal economic standards, this labour was grossly unprofitable. Seventeen men worked all winter to earn a few hundred Chinese dollars. But there was

46

nothing else they could do with their labour; it had no opportunity cost. The gain was all net gain and the members of the group who had earned it were pledged to save it and invest it. In this way they bought the simple tools necessary to begin co-operative farming.

In the work of farming they applied the same principle of investing very great labour in the intensification of cultivation to gain relatively small increases of output, and again most of the extra income was saved and invested in better tools, the acquisition of animal power, and the beginnings of diversification of the co-operative's operations into simple handicrafts.

Within three years, Wang Kuo-fan's co-operative was said to have an income per head as great as that of the more prosperous peasants who had refused to join it.

The truth or falsehood of this account of one co-operative is not the point, although as it became a demonstration farm it is unlikely that the account of its success is too distorted. Its point is in the dramatic vision it gives of the possibility that even the poorest in China might achieve prosperity by their own efforts through an economic process which, though it has never been made entirely explicit, is elaborated in considerable detail in the accounts of co-operatives given in the *High Tide*.

The point in this apparently uneconomic use of surplus labour power is not a belief that Chinese agriculture can be transformed simply by greater inputs of labour, without modern inputs such as chemical fertilizers. The point is that the small increases thus produced are net gain, and those who provide the labour are committed to save and invest a substantial part of this gain, to prime the pump of progress.

Almost any investment of labour, however, that can be made in farming itself or in the development of handicrafts, will increase the demand for labour for routine operations the following year. In doing so, it will fairly quickly produce a demand for labour-saving investment, even of a very simple type; in the poorer parts of rural China this may simply be the replacement of shoulder poles by wheel-barrows. The initial investment of surplus labour, however, will produce

47

not only the demand for labour-saving investment, but also the means.

If this labour-saving investment then increases the capacity of the co-operative to make further investments of labour in construction, and through this once more to increase incentives and savings for further labour-saving investment, then a spiral of development may be started in which Chinese agriculture may be mechanized, the rural economy diversified and eventually industrialized, and rural incomes brought up to urban levels. The means for development would come out of the pockets of the peasants themselves in a manner determined by the needs and the aspirations of the local community itself.

This can be done at a pace which they choose, according to these needs and according to their expanding resources, and by construction so phased that, generally speaking, the labour invested in this winter's off-season will pay off directly in increased production in the next harvest, so that the peasants are not obliged to commit resources over a long period during which they must sacrifiice a part of their already inadequate standard of living. And they will mechanize, in stages, only as and when increasing scarcities of labour are created.

This strategy was the basis of Mao's appeal to the Chinese peasants to organize agriculture in co-operative forms. The appeal was not couched in general terms, but in the form of inducing each village community to visualize these possibilities in terms of specific production plans, to which the community or a part of it then pledged themselves, and which were designed to maximize the use of their resources with the minimum of capital investment, usually taking in not only farming but auxiliary occupations. From the beginning, the Chinese co-operative farm was a community development project.

This economic strategy was closely linked to the gradualist method of collectivization adopted in China. Peasants were first encouraged to form mutual-aid teams in which the farmers continued to farm for their individual profit, but maximized mutual help on an agreed basis of exchange of labour or payment for labour. The second stage was the formation of a co-operative in which the individual peasants invested their land, receiving not only a return to the labour which they put in on the co-operative, but also a rent for their land. The final stage was the full collective, in which rent for land was no longer paid.

The process, however, was intended to be more smoothly gradualist than this schematization suggests. The mutual-aid teams were encouraged in the off-season of agriculture to participate in construction which would create common property, and to commit themselves to continuing co-operative enterprises which involved the acquisition of common assets. In this way, the members of a mutual-aid team might be brought to the point where the transition to the first level of co-operative agriculture was a natural one. The same encouragement to build up common property took place in the lower-level co-operatives. In addition, it was hoped that the proportion of co-operative income paid out in rent for land, as opposed to labour, could gradually be reduced and the proportion paid in wages increased, as the total income of the co-operative rose and as labour productivity rose (making the value of land a proportionately smaller input). The transition to the full collective could be made smoother and could be carried through in conditions of increasing production and incomes which would prevent more than a very small minority of the farmers involved from suffering any reduction of income in the process.

In the event, the final collectivization of Chinese agriculture was rushed and no time was given for the smooth operation of this process. Nevertheless, the collectivization of agriculture in China, although it was by no means entirely smooth, did not lead, as in Soviet Russia, to a virtual breakdown of the willingness and capacity of the farms to supply the towns; nor did it demand, as in Soviet Russia, the widespread use of coercion to maintain the farms in existence. This success was due to the economic strategy underlying collectivization in China and to the way in which Chinese villages were encouraged to apply this strategy for themselves by forming and carrying out their own production plans.

Meanwhile, experience of Russian-type industrial development during the First Five Year Plan was not entirely happy. China had been remarkably successful in developing heavy industry with Russian help. But this very success raised the problem that if a similar pace of development was to be maintained in a Second Five Year Plan, then agricultural production would have to develop much faster in order to provide the means of continuing industrialization. Chinese agriculture appears to have done quite well during the First Five Year Plan, but industry did much better. There was a vital gap in the rates of growth in the two main sectors of the economy. Agriculture, however, had been sufficiently successful that to achieve a higher rate of growth would require unprecedented measures.

At the same time, the population census of 1953 had shown a population one-quarter larger than had been estimated, with a heavy bias towards youth. It was clearly impossible for the State to provide jobs for more than a fraction of the young people coming on the labour market, not to mention doing this and also mopping up existing underemployment in the rural areas. Industry could only give limited help to agriculture, which would very largely have to help itself, and there was also the problem of maintaining a flow of consumers' goods to match increasing incomes in order to provide continuing incentives to agricultural and industrial workers alike.

In these circumstances Mao Tse-tung developed the economic ideas implicit in his collectivization strategy. He believed that by such means agricultural production could be improved, agriculture could be enabled to provide its own industrial overheads on a small local scale, and could take its first natural steps towards industrialization through the repair and manufacture of simple but improved tools and through the processing of crops; by this means, rural incomes could be increased, grain-deficient villages brought to self-sufficiency, the balance between the developed coast and the underdeveloped hinterland redressed, a flow of locally manufactured consumers' goods provided, the necessity of increased procurement of grain, etc. to increase funds for central invest-

50

ment avoided, and a vast range of new employment opportunities in the countryside provided without the heavy costs of urbanization and without further strain on central sources of capital.

Political Ideas

There was, however, a political dimension to the situation. The condemnation of Stalin by Khrushchev at the 20th Congress of the CPSU in 1956 had left the problem of what to put in place of Stalinism; the politics of Communist countries have been dominated by this ever since. This was a problem, but it was also an opportunity to reshape socialism. In Europe, with its parliamentary tradition, dissent had been almost entirely based on social-democratic ideas. In China, the same ideas were put forward vigorously during the Rectification Campaign, in which Mao Tse-tung asked for criticism of the régime. There was, however, another form of dissent in China—left-wing dissent. The target of right and left was the same, the centralized bureaucracy built up under Party control. The right wing saw its power as a denial of the civil rights and freedoms which the constitution of 1954 had promised. The left wing saw it as an obstacle to continued revolution. Mao Tse-tung chose to side with the left, who were in fact demanding the full implementation of mass-line methods. The left wing were freed to launch vigorous criticism against both the bureaucracy and the right-wing representatives of social democracy, and then to pass beyond criticism of individuals and ideas to the full application of mass-line techniques, including the economic strategy adumbrated in the *High Tide*, to provide a Maoist alternative to the Stalinist system of which Mao had, many years before, made oblique but trenchant criticisms.

This was the origin of the Great Leap Forward and the Communes. The theoretical basis, however, had already been laid in the speech, later published as a pamphlet, in which Mao had launched the Rectification Campaign—*On the Correct Handling of Contradictions Among the People*. In this, alluding to the discontent in Communist countries which

51

had culminated in the Hungarian Rising, Mao emphasized (as had never been emphasized before in Communist literature) the idea that conflicts could and would continue among the people of a socialist state; that is, even when antagonistic class conflicts had come to an end there would still be conflicts of interest and opinion which would have to be resolved. As these, however, were not antagonistic class contradictions, they could be resolved by education.

Mao was naturally particularly concerned with the conflict between the interests of peasants and the interests of industrial investment. He points out that the peasant's interest as an individual consumer conflicts with his interest as a member of the collective, which must accumulate for investment as well as consume; and his interest as a member of the collective conflicts with his interest as a member of the State, which again must draw from the production of collectives to provide means for central investment in industry and for the other tasks of the State. Mao of course insists that in the last analysis this an unreal conflict. Nevertheless, it is felt to be a conflict by the population and must be resolved.

At the end of the pamphlet Mao offers his solution: if the peasants are permitted and encouraged to develop industry for themselves at their own pace and in accordance with their own needs, then they will come to appreciate the vital relationship between industry and agriculture. In order that this should be possible, Mao advocated that instead of procurement norms and taxation being raised during the Second Five Year Plan to take advantage of the increased surplus of agriculture, their levels should be left as fixed in the First Five Year Plan, and the peasants—not as individuals but as collective communities—should be induced to invest a part of their increased incomes in the development of their own local economy.

The Re-shaping of Chinese Life

Gradually, and at a rapidly accelerating pace, Chinese life was reshaped for this purpose. The large centrally-controlled industrial establishments situated in the provinces were handed over to provincial control to serve as the backbone of the development of local industry at the county level and the village level. Central investment was given as its priority the creation of provincial centres of industry where these did not already exist, with the aim of having at least a first-stage complex of heavy industry in every provincial capital. In these industrial bases, priority was given to the production of the means of local and rural mechanization, electrification, and industrialization. The research-and-development departments of government ministries turned to producing blueprints of small-scale factories and industrial installations of all kinds, based usually on an intermediate technology which could be set up out of funds available to county governments and especially, at the smallest scale, out of the savings of Agricultural Producers' Co-operatives individually or in groups. A vast prospecting movement was organized to discover local sources of minerals, especially surface deposits of coal and iron ore. Millions of educated young people, technicians, and skilled workers, were put under pressure to go down to the localities and take their place in teams which also included members of the local collectives and local handicraftsmen, who could together work out improvements in existing farm tools and processes and in existing handicraft processes, including first-stage simple mechanization.

Great stress was put upon the possibilities of small-scale operations of this kind. It must not, however, be supposed that this policy represented some kind of populist, Ghandist preference for the dignity of human labour over the use of machines. On the contrary, the whole purpose of the Great Leap Forward was to set in motion a process which, beginning with the simple tools and hand processes available to the Chinese, and through this *High Tide* dialectic of an increasing demand for labour-saving innovation on the one hand and increasing means to pay for it on the other, would provide a spiral of local economic development which would eventually take the Chinese countryside to full employment, full mechanization, and full industrialization, and so would eliminate 'the three great differences'—between manual and mental labour, between town and country, and between industry and agriculture.

The Idea of Imbalance

From the beginning, the Great Leap Forward was criticized as an abdication of planning which could produce nothing but chaos. Mao Tse-tung's answer, however, dismissed the planners' obsession with balanced growth, insisted that imbalance is the normal state of the economy and that balance is only local and temporary. Typically, he also insisted that such imbalances—such contradictions—provided the motive force of economic development. He did not, therefore, see planned selective development as the antithesis of simultaneous spontaneous development, but on the other hand believed that the most effective dynamic balance would be reached if each community tried to maximize its resources in every possible way. In this process they would reach a sense of what the necessary key industrial developments in their area must be and where the bottle-necks occurred, and therefore would get together to pool their resources for the creation of such key enterprises.

Mao's contemptuous reference to China's economists as 'bookkeepers' expresses the fundamental difference between their approach to economics and his. He refuses to look at economic planning as a question of the arithmetical apportionment of fixed resources among a variety of tasks with differing priorities. On the contrary, he is concerned with the calling forth of latent resources. This was the principle on which the Great Leap Forward was based.

Gunnar Myrdal, in *Asian Drama*, points out that arguments among economists as to whether it is really possible to measure surplus labour are futile; that surplus labour in an under-developed community can only be measured in terms of a given set of policies. In other words, it is only when the problem of local development is posed that a local community has the incentive to use its labour to best advantage, and it is only then that labour resources can be effectively measured. The same principle applies to savings. It is only

54

when the community has made its mind up (in the manner in which a Chinese co-operative farm was supposed to make its mind up) as to what new possibilities exist, and how they can be taken advantage of, that the savings available in that community for investment can be measured. Without this planning, without new incentives, without new perspectives, these savings may not even exist.

Education Through Participation

The problem of calling forth such latent resources is essentially an educational one, and in a scattered, illiterate, and unsophisticated population, almost totally unaware of the possibilities of modern technology, this must be to a large extent education through participation. The Maoist spiral of local economic development, therefore, has a necessary educational dimension. It can be described as a process which aims to develop consciousness of the possibility of control and exploitation of the natural world.

The Relations of Politics and Economics

Mao's ideas of economic development have not been readily appreciated by Western economists because the factors to which he attaches most importance are not those readily quantifiable, and economists deal largely in what can be quantified. To Mao Tse-tung, the process of economic development in a poor country is a process of radicalization of thought and practice, no different in nature from the processes of political radicalization. Questions of the kind which economists deal with, concerned with efficient allocation of resources, are to Mao not only secondary, but derivative.

Economic ideas are therefore analogous to political ideas; moreover, they are closely linked. In so far as developing consciousness in the economic sphere is liable to inhibition by political influences, especially by the class interests of those (be they landlords, rich peasants, capitalist employers, or Communist officials and Party members) who are doing well out of the existing system, then politics is relevant to economics. If it is important for the poor majority to feel that the administrative machine, or the factory or commune management, is clearly directed to serving their interests and supporting their efforts, then politics is obviously relevant to economics. Politics must 'take command' of the economy; it may be that the final authority in a factory or a commune should therefore be the politicians (the Party committee or the revolutionary committee) rather than the professional manager or the technicians.

Mao's ideas appear to have been shared by all or most of the Chinese Communist Party, or were at least acceptable to all, during the first decade of Communist rule. Only in 1959, after the Great Leap Forward and the Commune movement, were they for the first time subjected to criticism.

The idea of the Great Leap, however, was by no means irrational. The history of the non-Communist Chinese Industrial Co-operatives of the Second World War had already shown how modern industries might be built out of virtually nothing by a process starting with simple techniques on a small scale, and developing as the workers themselves gained the experience necessary to improve processes, build better machines, and expand the scale of management.

These co-operatives of the 1940s already had Great Leap Forward perspectives. They had also shown that in the conditions of the Chinese countryside, any new enterprise, no matter what it was set up to produce, found it necessary to diversify in order to create its own social overheads, to secure its own raw material supplies, and even to supply its own power. More than this, many of these enterprises found it necessary to set up a school because their workers were illiterate, and to set up a clinic or a hospital because of the low standards of health prevailing in conditions of under-nourishment. In these circumstances, co-operatives often spread until they were absorbing the entire surplus labour and resources of a whole village—and at this stage, the Industrial Co-operative had become virtually a Commune. Mao was familiar with these wartime co-operatives, learned from them in Yenan, and expressed his admiration for them and gratitude to them in 1942.

The same considerations applied in China in 1958 as in 1940; the problems had not changed, the modernization of the Chinese rural economy had by no means (as the right wing of the Chinese Communist Party was later to argue) reached the stage when a modern 'rational' division of labour and resources planned from above could solve the problems which any single new enterprise would face: 'simultaneous development' was still essential.

The Commune

The Commune (thus foreshadowed by the wartime co-operatives under Rewi Alley, the New Zealand pioneer of Chinese industrialization) provided the institutional framework of the Great Leap Forward. Consisting of from ten to twenty adjacent collective farms brought into a single unit and merged with the *hsiang* (rural district) government, it created on the basis of the *hsiang* a new economic and social unit, responsible not only for farming and agricultural construction and for the development of local industry, but for government, education, and welfare, all of which were now to be organized in a close mutual relationship by the elected council of the Commune. The new Commune unit was large enough for effective mobilization of local labour, effective use of local resources, and effective concentration of local savings by bringing poor and prosperous villages into a single unit of account. At the same time, it was small enough to permit a high degree of democratic participation in its government.

The Commune was the culmination of Mao's mass-line ideas. The economic policies it was created to serve had an ancestry going back through the community-development strategy of the collectivization campaigns to the co-operative land reclamation of the Border Regions, and to the Chinese Industrial Co-operatives. In its political aspect, it was meant to be Mao's final solution to the problems created by the Soviet-type centralized bureaucracy condemned in the Rectification Movement of 1957 by both right and left. The Great Leap Forward and the Commune movement were indeed

57

explicitly defended as a direct and natural consequence of popular resistance to bureaucracy and 'bourgeois attitudes' in 1957; the masses, involved in criticism of bureaucratism and élitism, swept on beyond this to create their own mass-line alternative.

The balance between local initiative and central direction which the Commune system attempted was characteristic of Mao's thought, and in particular of his dialectical view of such contradictions. Instead of an administrative compromise between local freedom of decision-making and central direction, Mao sought to 'transcend' this contradiction—to secure a new synthesis in which both freedom and direction would be effectively increased, because they would feed each other and not fight each other. The means was to substitute for the maximization of control the maximization of communication. Local communities, organized in the Communes, would make their own plans and pursue them; the organs of government would watch over the process, provide the broad ideological limits, give full national publicity to the best local results, throw the weight of provincial and central resources into the solution of the most critical imbalances, rationalize the whole mass of local efforts into a dynamic national movement propagated through the developing mass media, and help to maintain the impetus of progress by pointing out and analysing the new problems which every new success created.

In conception, the campaigns of 1958 were the most inspiring attempt at total war on poverty which the world has seen, and the most generous attempt yet made in any poor country to create planned social change and economic development on the basis of popular aspirations and of the latent talents of ordinary people. The West, however, treated the whole movement with derision, giving full publicity to every example of the marginal extravagances which were the inevitable accompaniment of a movement which roused the impassioned hopes of millions of poor and simple people. The left wing in Europe at the same time did the Chinese a disservice by ignoring its practical basis as thoroughly as the right, and praising the movement for ideological reasons which, though they played some part in the arguments by which Mao sought to persuade the Chinese people to participate, did not and could not clearly convey the underlying realities to a foreign audience.

Criticism and Hostility

When in late 1958 and 1959 a right-wing opposition to the movement developed in China, the Western critics seemed to have been justified. When China plunged into three years of bad harvests, near-famine, and consequent industrial stagnation, China's enemies abroad rejoiced and hailed the imminent collapse of the régime.

The truth, however, was much more complex. It was largely obscured when the right wing in China won the struggle, slowed down the Great Leap, and abolished the Communes in all but name. Criticisms of the movement out of the mouths of Chinese Communist leaders themselves seemed to be a clinching argument that Western criticism had been right. But before we hasten to accept this point of view, two things must be considered; first, that the criticisms made by the right wing in China were as polemical as the earlier left-wing defence of the movement and cannot be taken at their face value; and second, that a coincidence of views between Westerners who accept uncritically the idea that society and economic life must inevitably be dominated by a managerial élite, and the Chinese managerial élite threatened by the Great Leap, is no proof of anything. The non élitist alternative could still be right, and it is interesting that during the following decade conventional élitist assumptions were increasingly attacked in the West.

The criticisms of the Great Leap made by the Chinese right wing marked a new and vital division in the Chinese leadership. Until 1958, there seemed to be a general acceptance of the basic tenets of Maoism. We can see now, however, that the mass line had meant different things to different people, although only the radical, comprehensive application of the Maoist interpretation in 1958 revealed to us—and perhaps indeed to the Chinese themselves—how profound

59

these differences were. There is all the difference in the world between the idea that the decision-making group must consult the people and take their points of view into consideration, and the idea that the people themselves must make the decision with the help and advice of their leaders. It is not an unfamiliar difference; it is an unresolved conflict in all systems which are in fact or in theory democratic.

The right wing in China crystallized out on this issue, finding support in a variety of places—among Party leaders whose former experiences had been mainly within the hierarchical Party apparatus, among those whose power and responsibilities had been based on planning from above, among the managers in industry (many of them the former private owners of the enterprises) and among those peasants who believed that they could find greater opportunities outside the collective than inside it by producing for the private market.

The objections of these groups to the Commune system and the Great Leap were various. They argued that the attempt at simultaneous development produced a chaos of scarcities and surpluses and jammed the transport system. They believed that the attempt to ensure a basic livelihood to all who worked on the Commune by a 'free supply' system would injure working incentives. They deplored the progressive escalation of production targets during the Great Leap, and thought that the handing over of China's existing resources of agricultural machinery to the Communes to use as they saw fit had occasioned losses rather than gains. They held that the Commune was too large (and too impersonal) a unit for day-to-day agriculture. They were convinced that the almost complete absorption of the private sector into communal ownership had grossly damaged peasant incentives for only marginal gains. Finally, they believed that the whole policy had been pushed through with too much haste.

Some of these charges Mao Tse-tung was explicitly or implicitly to accept, and in some cases he acknowledged his own responsibility for the decisions involved. He emphasized that the Commune idea was his personal responsibility, but he added that the incredible haste with which the communization of China was carried through was not his responsibility; he put the blame for that on certain provincial leaders and certain journalists. Since the Cultural Revolution, it has become clear that Mao and the left wing accept that to concentrate ownership and direct management at the Commune level rather than to distribute them as appropriate between the Commune and its sub-divisions was premature, if not actually mistaken. They accept that the private sector should not have been immediately abolished but gradually brought under control. They accept that the escalation of targets was forced at an unrealistic pace.

But, as we shall see below, they still insist that on balance the Great Leap was creative and effective, that the Commune is the social unit of the future, if not of the present, and that the basic strategy underlying the Great Leap is the best strategy for China. They defend themselves by charging that the right wing, while in theory accepting the Great Leap, 'sabotaged' it by reluctance to accept it in practice; the planners who should have rationalized the total effort refused to see anything in it but an intractable mess, and those who should have advised and helped the Communes in the development and operation of mechanized farming did nothing.

The precise truth may never be known about these controversies; as for the practical consequences of the movement, they are very difficult to estimate as, by the very nature of the movement, good statistical records could not be kept. The three bad years which followed have also obscured the picture; and we cannot even be certain how far these bad years were due simply to adverse weather, and how far they were due, either to a drastic fall in incentives in agriculture, or to a labour scarcity produced by the too rapid encouragement of employment opportunities outside agriculture, or both. China's recovery, moreover, was based to some extent (disputed inside the Communist Party) upon a *sauve-qui-peut* restoration of private enterprise in the countryside to the point, at least in some places, that collectivized agriculture had broken down and family farming had reappeared with the approval of some of the leadership.

61

New Policies

By 1962, with economic recovery, the breach seemed to have been healed. The 10th Plenum of the 8th Central Committee announced new policies. The three principal new slogans, taken together, indicated that the Maoists had won a victory. 'Agriculture the foundation, heavy industry the leading factor' indicated that the 1958 policy of gearing industrial development primarily to the rapid development of agriculture had been re-asserted. 'Mechanization, electrification, irrigation, and chemical fertilizers' indicated the lines on which agricultural development was to proceed. 'The class struggle must continue' indicated that socialism in the countryside was to be re-asserted against the more prosperous peasants who had deserted the socialized sector, as the necessary basis of the full mobilization of rural resources for the vast programme now undertaken. On this basis, a Socialist Education Movement was launched to restore collectivized agriculture. It continued with varying success and varying results until the Cultural Revolution of 1966.

In these years, however, the breach between left and right actually opened wider. The conclusions of the 10th Plenum could be interpreted in very different ways, and while Mao was elaborating his own interpretation in the form of the restoration of mass-line enterprise, Liu Shao-ch'i appears to have been equally busy in formulating for the first time a fully elaborated alternative on the lines of the reform of political and economic control then being carried out in the Soviet Union and Eastern Europe.

The clash came, perhaps predictably, over the best means to mechanize agriculture. By 1965, Liu was in favour of putting the manufacture and operation of farm machinery in an autonomous national trust explicitly modelled, as far as internal organization is concerned, on Western capitalist trusts. This would operate tractor stations on a profit-making basis, the profits to be used for further development of agricultural machines.

Mao vehemently opposed this policy. Committed to low procurement norms and low taxation, he would not contemplate state-controlled centralized development which would inevitably mean an increase in taxation, direct or concealed. Committed to the development of the more backward areas of China, he opposed a policy which would mean (in the pursuit of profit) the concentration of resources for mechanized farming in those parts of China already more developed and more prosperous. Passionately convinced that economic development was largely a problem of education in new possibilities, he saw little prospect of any educational effect in the rural areas from the operation of machinery by urban engineers for short periods on each farm each year. He insisted, reverting to his *High Tide* theory of local development, that the farms could be most quickly and effectively mechanized by inducing a process of gradual mechanization on the basis of local needs and local resources.

Perhaps the hottest issue is the most revealing: Liu apparently stipulated that the centres of mechanized agriculture (his tractor stations) should be so distributed as to ensure that they would be independent of the local communities. To Mao and his supporters, however, the first necessity was precisely that existing resources should be put at the disposal of the local communities to use as freely and as fully they could; this was the basic premise of Maoist development strategy.

The Cultural Revolution

It was partly in reaction to the elaboration of the Liuist alternative that the Cultural Revolution was launched in 1965 and 1966.

On September 3, 1965, Lin Piao, who had replaced Peng Teh-huai, the most outspoken critic of the Commune system, as the chief of the People's Liberation Army, made a speech on defence and foreign policy, in which he openly came out against those who favoured a renewal of the alliance with the Soviet Union, as the price of the arms necessary to halt what was feared would be the escalation of war in Vietnam to the point of an American invasion of south China. This issue between those who believed that China could be defended only with modern weapons, modern transport, and air cover—

63

and therefore only with Soviet help—and those who believed that China could defend herself, in independence, by a 'people's war', was by no means the least important of the divisive issues in Chinese politics, though with the beginnings of the American retreat from intervention in Vietnam, it was very soon to lose its urgency. More important, Mao seems to have taken Lin Piao's speech as a signal that Lin Piao would support his policies generally; and certainly since his assumption of office Lin had used all his influence to build up the personal prestige of Mao Tse-tung in the armed forces, so providing a means by which Mao could regain his dominant influence and carry out the policies in which he so strongly believed.

At any rate, immediately after this speech, the first round was fired in the Cultural Revolution: the anti-Maoist play by Wu Han, *The Dismissal of Hai Jui,* was criticized in unmeasured terms in a Shanghai newspaper. The attack then spread to the anti-Maoist satirists in Peking's evening newspaper, and when their patron, P'eng Chen (Communist leader of Peking and a possible claimant to the succession when the ageing Mao should die) resisted these attacks, he was turned out of office. From there the attacks spread to those in charge of education, publicity, and propaganda, who, Mao believed, had willingly acted as the apologists for those whom he regarded as a 'new bourgeoisie' (the 'royalists', as they were now called) who favoured Liu Shao-ch'i's East-European liberal solution to China's political and economic problems.

P'eng Chen's patronage of the satirists of the Peking *Evening News* was one reason for his downfall, which marked the point where the Cultural Revolution became a struggle for power. But of equal, perhaps greater importance, was his part in the controversy over the mechanization of Chinese agriculture, revived by new, Maoist, policy proposals drafted by the Hupeh Provincial Party, and commented on marginally by Mao himself. P'eng Chen took his red pencil through this document on behalf of the Central Committee, changed it substantially, and had the temerity to cut out some of Mao's own marginal comments, including his criticism of Soviet agricultural policy. The latent differences between Mao and the right wing of the Party on this issue—an issue both vital in itself and symbolic of the whole range of differences in attitude and policy between the two sides—was now fully exposed.

The attack was pressed home, inside the Party itself particularly, by newly formed 'cultural revolution committees' which sought to force the Party committees at all levels to submit fully to public criticism. Liu Shao-ch'i as head of state and Teng Hsiao-p'ing as head of the Party apparatus resisted this, and sought to prevent the washing of dirty linen in public, by putting the reform of the Party in the hands of Party work teams. It was because of this that the Cultural Revolution swung from attacks primarily directed at the apparatus of publicity and the formation of opinion, to attacks on the Liu Shao-ch'i administration itself.

The students of Peking University had taken the lead in the attack, which spread throughout China, on conservative teachers and administrators. Mao now published in Peking University his own 'big character poster'—a wall newspaper item— demanding that the target be changed to 'those in power', which can be quite accurately translated as 'the establishment'. The students' attack swung round on the very Party leaders who had been stumping the country (though only with varying degrees of enthusiasm) organizing student protest against the educational authorities.

The Red Guards, who appeared for the first time in mid-August, 1966, at a giant rally in Peking, wearing the red arm-bands of the revolutionary militia of the old Kiangsi Soviet, became the student spearhead of protest against the establishment. Their activities, attacking every symbol of conservative vestiges, taking over police headquarters, newspaper offices, and broadcasting stations, invading government offices to expose their secret files, invading the factories to harangue the workers (who, with their incentive bonuses at risk and their trade unions put out of action, were not at first disposed to listen and often ejected the students with some violence), reduced urban China to chaos and confusion and paralysed administration. The chaos was made worse by mutual hostility among the various Red Guard groups.

Deprived of Party leadership, they had to form their own leadership and provide their own interpretation of Mao's occasional brief statements, and the movement splintered into warring factions.

Mao Tse-tung appealed to the armed forces under Lin Piao, less in order to secure their armed intervention (though this was occasionally necessary) than to make use of them as the most effectively indoctrinated and best organized part of the Left. Their duty was to persuade the radicals to compromise and unite, rather than to suppress dissent by force.

Gradually the situation was brought under control again. Liu Shao-ch'i was dismissed from office as head of state. Province by province, revolutionary committees composed of representatives of 'the masses' (the left-wing protesters), the People's Liberation Army, and those cadres who had not been dismissed or demoted, were formed. They represented an alliance among these groups: Mao with his radical supporters; Lin Piao's troops, who though personally loyal to Mao did not necessarily as soldiers subscribe to Mao's tolerance of unsoldierly mess while people were learning to act for themselves; and Chou En-lai, who though a sincere supporter of Mao's ideas, had the responsibility of preserving an intact and continuing administrative machine.

Three years of struggle, propaganda, and political manoeuvring followed, during which the most vocal man of the extreme left, Ch'en Po-ta (a very close personal associate of Mao) fell from office, and Lin Piao, after a prolonged struggle behind the scenes to prevent the indefinite perpetuation of army dominance, also disappeared. This left the moderate Maoists headed by Chou En-lai apparently in supreme control. Mao had taken the lid off Chinese politics, and courted chance to find a solution. He had ridden a tiger which he himself had loosed, and ridden it until he tamed it. Put on the shelf as a 'lacquered image' in 1959, he had made the best of this position as an idol to stage a melodramatic political come-back.

The stage was now set for the restoration of mass-line policies, though more cautiously applied than in 1958 and 1959.

A Provisional Evaluation

It is too soon yet to judge the effectiveness of Mao's policies as a whole; yet some provisional evaluation can be made. It seems likely from the unbroken run of good harvests which China has enjoyed since 1962 that, in spite of their faults, the mass-line campaigns of local irrigation and flood control of 1958 and 1959, renewed again after 1962, have given China far greater agricultural stability than before.

In the absence of adequate national statistics, it is also obvious that, while we cannot easily judge China's total industrial achievements, there has been since 1958 a remarkable diversification of Chinese products which has given Chinese industry a versatility and flexibility unknown in comparable countries.

It seems clear that in the better communes, the campaigns of 1958 for the development of local industry, though they ran into difficulties at first, have eventually produced the intended result. Almost all Chinese villages now have electricity, and in about two-thirds of cases this is the result of the use of small generators bought by the local community. In the supply of chemical fertilizers, the cost of the transport of which is a major limiting factor in their use, China has made a break-through of universal importance in the small-scale local manufacture of nitrates. Everywhere in China there is a very great diversity of local, semi-mechanized industry, and in factories at the county level this has already developed to the point of virtually complete modernization. All of this has been done largely out of the resources of the people themselves, with only marginal state help.

In the political sphere, the least that can be said is that the Chinese revolution, unlike other revolutions, has not, even after a generation, produced a new ruling class of 'red bourgeoisie'; the revolution is still popular and open-ended. Whether Mao's 'rectification' techniques and mass-line organization will eventually succeed in preventing the formation of a privileged élite may be doubted; but there seems at least a far greater possibility of success in China than elsewhere, and if the new education system is successful in pro-

67

viding equality of opportunity in practice as well as in theory, the problem may be solved. At any rate, there is general agreement that ordinary Chinese people have lost, at least in their personal manners, the traits of dependency: they are forthright, relaxed, and articulate as never before; and it seems possible therefore that they will soon be in a better position to defend their interests from, and to impose their opinions on, the educated minority whose talents even Mao accepts are necessary for the running and the development of China.

Whether or not the administration of communes and factories has been successfully democratized we do not know; but one can point to the changes that have taken place in medical services, scientific priorities, and education, as evidence of considerable success in putting specialized talents firmly in the service of the majority; and one can observe in the new village-based social security provisions a leap forward in social conscience which must be significant for the future.

It would be a paradox if this régime, avowedly totalitarian, dictatorial, and repressive as it is, were to teach the democratic West how to organize a truly participating democracy. Yet the very magnitude of China's peculiar problems—élitism, hierarchy, the distaste for conflict, bureaucratic assumptions—may well have forced the Chinese under Mao Tse-tung to radical measures which may drive them ahead of the West in some vital respects at least, on the road to a more just and in a real sense a more free society, in spite of the strict limits put to freedom of opinion and freedom of action outside the revolutionary concensus represented by Mao's thought.

These limits are not, however, limits of dogma so much as limits implicit in prescriptions for proper action; for Maoism is less a system of political belief than a mode of political action.

If we return to the question with which the chapter began: has Mao in his old age lost his grip on reality and become an impotent dreamer, a moralizing idealogue ready to sacrifice the material progress which is China's first need, to dream of moral consistency?

Perhaps this chapter has suggested an answer. Maoism may be right or wrong: there is no logic and no calculus which can give us an indisputable answer. But whether right or wrong, it does not seem to be irrational; its practical applications are so fully elaborated that one can be in no doubt of what it means, and in no doubt that it is relevant to China's problems. It represents at least half the truth about China.

So far from representing the stubborn adherence of an old man to ideas no longer relevant, it is clear that Maoism (though the basic ideas have not changed) has developed as the situation in China has developed, in demonstrable and plausible relationship to this changing situation.

So far from representing a willingness to sacrifice material progress to moral dreams, Maoism is emphatically concerned with material progress; but Mao believes that no society which is unjust can be efficient, that only when society operates and is seen to operate in the interests of the majority can the energies and talents of that majority be harnessed to progress. This is his faith, and it is a faith which has its roots not in Soviet Communism, but in the intuitions of his early years, when he discovered what was common ground between Western democrats who stressed the creative value of free individual development, and Marx' concern for and pity for the 'alienated' of exploited societies.

3

THE RELEVANCE OF MAOISM

ALL political theory grows out of practical experience, which must mean largely the experience of a particular place and time. Even the political thinker who, like Mao Tse-tung himself, believes he is prescribing for the whole human race and for all time, has actually started from a compelling need to cope with a definite and obvious crisis of his own society in his own generation. This is as true of Mao as of Macchiavelli. Not only must we see Mao's thought as a reaction to his country's desperate situation in the twentieth century, but we have even been able to point to the year and to the event which first forced him to think out his ideas fully and to express them systematically—the Japanese retaliation for the Hundred Regiments Offensive of June, 1940. And in Mao's case, as in the case of Macchiavelli, if his new ideas should prove to be of more than temporary and local relevance, if they should prove to be of universal value, this is incidental.

Political and social thought, however, is not local only in the problems which a writer feels compelled to solve. It is also usually local in its means of expression. Every thinker will use the concepts, language, and tools of analysis which are to hand, choosing from these whichever seem best suited to his purpose, and employing them until their usefulness for this purpose is exhausted. Only then will he use new concepts and often he will only resort to the creation of such new concepts after the meaning of his inherited concepts has been twisted to the utmost to serve his new purpose.

The questions which must therefore be asked about every political thinker are:

70

What were the problems in his own society which he sought to solve?

What concepts, language, and tools of analysis were already available to him for the solution of these problems?

Which of these concepts did he employ unchanged and which of them was he forced to emphasize, expand, or distort?

What new concepts, if any, was he obliged to employ to make his arguments good?

Having answered these questions, we may then choose to make the judgment that his thought is only 'historically interesting'—that is, that it has no great relevance to anything outside the thinker's own place and time. On the other hand, we may make the judgment that in trying to solve the problems under his hand, he has provided solutions which, in whole or part, in spirit or in detail, have added to humanity's general stock of wisdom and self-knowledge; in a word, that his ideas have the quality of universality.

In China

The problems which Maoism seeks to solve are conventionally divided into two different categories representing two different periods: those involved in seizing revolutionary power and those involved in the construction of socialist society. There are two good reasons, one particular and one general, for rejecting such a division. The particular reason is that Mao Tse-tung and his associates within the Chinese Communist Party have been in power since 1927, when the Kiangsi Soviet was first created, in conditions which dictated that seizure of national power was only possible on the basis of constructive changes in the society of the areas of China which they held.

The more general reason springs from the fact that Communist régimes have nowhere fulfilled the prediction of Marx that the Communist revolution would take place in the most advanced capitalist societies. Revolutions have in fact taken place in poor and backward countries. This has changed the whole original Marxist conception of the revo-

71

lution. The building up of the economy to the levels represented by advanced capitalism must now take place after, instead of before, the revolution. Instead of an advanced economic base producing of necessity an advanced social and cultural superstructure, the 'advanced' elements in the superstructure—that is, radical intellectuals, usually of middle-class origin, with the support of such urban workers as may be present—must set about creating a new economic base. Therefore, the creation of socialist political consciousness from above is a condition both of the successful seizure of power and of the construction of socialism. These conditions applied in the Soviet Union. Given, however, that China was much poorer than Russia, and much more backward in every measureable and relevant respect (including the fact that the state had not reached the point of effective centralization, and so there was no centre of power whose seizure would be decisive on a national scale), the seizure and maintenance of power (local power in revolutionary base areas) depended upon increased political consciousness induced by successful social change. In the same way, the formal seizure of power at a national level in 1949 has been succeeded, step by step through land reform, economic planning and socialization, the Commune system and the Great Leap Forward, and finally the Cultural Revolution, by the repeated re-assertion of revolutionary power, each time upon the basis of a new pattern of social forces. The seizure of power and the reform of society cannot be divided in Chinese Communist practice.

There is another dimension to the consequences of the fact that Communist revolutions have not taken place in advanced countries. The Bolshevik leaders in 1917 were confident that in the aftermath of the First World War the capitalist countries of Western Europe would undergo revolution. They did not, and the Communist leaders of Russia were forced to seek other allies where they could. Lenin evolved the theory that because of the effects of economic imperialism, the potential for revolution had shifted from the advanced capitalist countries to the colonial and semi-colonial world. There the subjugated peoples felt the full weight of capitalist oppression and the full force of the example of the prosperity of their colonial rulers. Consequently, it was argued, the populations of the poor world beyond Europe would be the first to be radicalized. The middle classes of these countries would provide the first resistance against imperialism, and would become the first leaders of the revolution, with the Communist-led workers and peasants as their allies. This theory justified Communists in allying with national bourgeois movements and even accepting for the time being a subordinate position to the middle classes. This was the rationale for the alliance between the Chinese Communists and the Chinese National Party from 1924 to 1927. The alliance, as we have seen, ended in Chiang K'ai-shek's coup in Shanghai in April, 1927, and in disaster for the Communists, but it was revived when the Communist Party had reached a position of strength from which it could dictate the terms of a coalition of nationalist and radical elements, whose formal basis was Mao's *New Democracy*. Broadly speaking, Mao's policies have since then followed out this Leninist perspective.

It is clear, therefore, that analysis of the problems of radical change in China, as seen by Chinese Communists, could, without too much inconsistency, be expressed in the language of Leninism. Mao has had no need to strive for new formulations, and given the nature of the audience—a Communist Party audience—to which most of his writings have been addressed, he has had every reason to avoid departure from the Communist mode of expression. If Mao's writings are taken phrase by phrase, it is easy to demonstrate that, phrase by phrase, they have no originality. But such a mode of analysis reveals nothing except the poverty-stricken notions of intellectual development entertained by the analyst. For the first rule of intellectual history is that the same idea may bear an entirely different meaning in a different situation. To understand the originality of Mao Tse-tung, we must accept that his most original ideas have usually had to be expressed in a language turned stale and sour in Western democratic minds by its association with the violent excesses and the intellectual vacuity of Stalin. Only when Mao is appealing to the Chinese people as a whole does he break these bonds of linguistic convention and reveal the richness of his mind, but usually to express himself in metaphor or in epigram rather than in argument.

The Chinese situation which Mao describes in Russian terms differs from the Russian situation of 1917 at least in degree, in that those problems of revolution in a poor country which forced Lenin to bend Marxist analysis to new and un-expected purposes are even greater to the degree that China's poverty is greater. It may be that this difference in degree is so great as to amount to a difference in kind. At Chinese levels of income, there could be no question of realizing the capital for development by tightening peasants' belts. There could be no question of basing a revolution on the political strength of the urban proletariat, which in China was in-signficant in numbers. In an economy too little commer-cialized to have produced a high degree of polarization in society, the problem was not merely the successful organizing of existing radical forces, but their creation by a process of radicalization of thought. There could be no question of changing Chinese society from above, either by legislation or coercion, in a country in which power lay in the villages.

The Chinese situation was further complicated from the point of view of radical leaders by the special features of China's own traditional and social behaviour, upon which we have already touched—the long tradition of élitism, the accep-tance of heirarchy and the consequent inability to co-operate with equals, and the fear of conflict. In these circumstances, conventional Marxist slogans, when used to attack these traditional Chinese attitudes, mean something very different from their original meaning as applied to situations in the Soviet Union produced by the greater aggressiveness of Europeans, the impulsiveness of the Russian character, and the factiousness engendered in the Russian radical leadership by long years of exile and impotence. It has been in fighting Chinese tradition rather than by perpetuating it that Maoism has diverged from the orthodox Soviet model.

Just as traditional Chinese behaviour has in this way posed new problems for Communist theory and practice, so the very different nature of Chinese society in those respects to which we have already alluded posed very different problems.

If, as we have just argued, Maoism is so largely a response to the specific conditions of China, a real sinification of Marxism, then it might be that the thought of Mao Tse-tung is valuable only for China, and is of no interest and can have no application outside the Chinese context. This is the question we must now attempt to answer.

In Developing Countries

If we look broadly at the problems which Maoism seeks to solve, it is obvious, first, that many of these problems are shared by many under-developed countries; second, that many of them are problems for advanced countries also; and third, that many of these problems in China which have been created by Communist organization itself, usually associated with the bureaucratic results of one-Party rule, are shared by all Communist countries.

The best way to illustrate the possible relevance of Maoist ideas and policies to the problems of other poor countries is to look again briefly at Mao's economic programme, which is based on the use of surplus labour not only to replace capital, but to create it. It operates through the incentives which the local community finds in creating its own enterprises for its own agreed purposes. It is intended partly to solve the problem of an increasing population and in particular the difficulty of providing employment for the vast numbers of young people who come on the labour market every year. It solves this problem by creating industry on the basis of local needs, in the rural localities, with two obvious advantages—that rural labour, surplus for most of the year but in short supply at sowing and harvest, can be employed on the spot in the off-seasons, and that the costs of urbanization incidental to orthodox large-scale industrialization can be avoided.

It seeks also by this means to stem the flow of peasants looking for employment in the cities. Urban industry is geared largely to providing the necessary modern backbone for the creation of an intermediate technology, which is cheap enough for local communities to afford, and simple enough for them to operate. Local development is so phased as to minimize gestation periods, with (in principle) what is done this winter paying off at the next harvest so that long-term reductions in consumption are not necessary. Development takes place through a process of education through participation, which can deal with the psychological and social obstacles to change.

One consequence hoped for from this process is that as new possibilities open out to the local peasant community, they will provide surplus labour and savings which might otherwise never be mobilized. The unit of development (the three-level commune) is large enough for effective planning, and flexible enough to allow different tasks to be carried out on the most efficient scale, and small enough to make popular participation in decision-making possible.

This system seeks to avoid or to redress historical regional differences of income and resources, through local self-reliance. It renders less necessary the maintenance of a large bureaucratic and technocratic machine which might evolve into a privileged class, and brings the maximum number of such state functionaries directly into the service of local communities and into constant contact with them as advisers, not commanders. It seeks also, through local diversification and industrialization, eventually to abolish the paralysing gulf between city and country.

There is no need to go into a lengthy exposition to demonstrate that every problem which Maoist strategy thus seeks to meet exists in the under-developed countries generally, and that the solution he offers is the most systematic in existence. It is impossible at present to judge whether it has succeeded or failed. What can be said, however, is that most hostile Western comment upon it has been based on out-of-date prejudices about our own society's workings, or on the gross ignorance of most Western intellectuals of the practical facts of Western industry and agriculture.

The first naïve assumption of hostile Western commentators is that collective incentives, as opposed to individual incentives, cannot be effective. This is an *a priori* argument that

76

cannot be sustained. British coal-mining, for example, is and always has been based on collective incentives: every man digging coal at the face loads eventually into the same carriages, and the total earnings from the day's work are divided equally; and yet the working morale of miners is probably higher than that of the workers of any other British industry.

Many commentators, taking Maoist epigrams in too literal a sense, affirm that Mao believes that any sort of material incentive is morally wrong, and refuses to provide it. This is not in fact the case. Incentives to pursue private individual enterprise on the private plot or in the private market are subjected to control; incentives directly relating remuneration to work done, in the form of piecework payments, are roundly condemned, and rightly—all experience shows that piecework in farming, as practised in Soviet Russia, is grossly inefficient, and even in industry in advanced countries is a poor substitute for a conscientious labour force willing to give a fair week's work for a fixed wage. But Mao has always insisted on the importance of material incentives in general, insisting that no policy aimed at social and economic change is likely to succeed unless it produces a rise in personal income.

The attack on Mao's belief that material incentives alone are of limited value is based on simple ignorance of all the studies made in the West for the last generation on work motivation. No industrial sociologist or industrial psychologist would now maintain that material incentives constitute more than one factor in working attitudes. Pride in the job, a sense of identity and personal significance which comes from co-operation in a productive enterprise, are of far greater importance. Moreover, it is obvious that where workers do lay stress on material incentives, it is in industries in which their opportunities to take pride in their work, and to develop a sense of responsibility, have been destroyed or minimized by bad management. We still do not know what the balance of motives for work would be in a firm which accepted that a man's work place is the real centre of his adult social life, and organized it as such, as Mao seeks to do.

77

Attacks of a similar kind on Mao's condemnation of bureaucratic management of industry are based on similar ignorance, on the assumption that Western and Soviet paramilitary staff-line management is the only possible form of management in modern industry. Such opinions show, in the first place, complete ignorance of the chronic problems and gross inefficiences of modern management of this kind, of which every executive in big business is aware. The recent literature of Western industrial management wholly supports the belief that a cumbersome bureaucratic apparatus is needed only in proportion as the workers are barred from taking responsibility. It is just as clear that production as well as morale is improved by 'job enlargement' that is, by giving each worker the largest practicable range of work—a conclusion that echoes Mao's insistence on the value of versatility.

Comment on the question of large-scale industry versus small-scale industry is similarly based upon ignorance. No economist would dispute that scale involves increased costs as well as increased savings; and few economists would assert that there is only one optimum scale for each industry in all economic circumstances. The different local price of labour, capital, and resources, the availability of skills, and the costs of transport all influence the choice of scale and of technology. In the real world (and more especially in a huge, varied, backward country with undeveloped communications, like China) there is therefore a whole range of possible choices.

The problem, however, goes deeper than this; it is by no means proved for all industries, or even for most industries, that technology dictates large-scale management. It may well be that pressures in Western and Soviet society towards large-scale management and centralization may often determine the choice of technology. Often, among economic as opposed to social factors, it is the needs of marketing and research which dictate the scale of management or of ownership rather than the needs of production—marketing because of its importance in a competitive consumer society; research because we choose to carry on such research as part of business rather than through government or academic agencies; a substantial part of such research is, in any case, connected more with marketing than with real technical innovation. There is, in addition, ample evidence that new products and new processes tend to be launched, not by large firms, but by small firms on very small capital.

Thus it is clear that none of the arguments used against these aspects of Maoism is convincing. It is equally clear that in tackling problems of incentives and work motivitation, of management and participation, and of choice of technique and choice of scale, Mao is dealing in China with problems which are also important for both other developing countries and advanced countries.

The same relationship between China's problems and our own applies in questions of social policy as in those aspects of the economy described above. The re-organization of the Chinese medical profession in order to change its priorities from the continued creation of a profession of highly-trained doctors serving in the cities, to the provision of simple medical services throughout the rural population and the dissemination of knowledge of hygiene, with peripatetic doctors seeking to leave behind them in each village the beginnings of a clinic and a nursing service, is a type of policy now widely advocated, and in some measure implemented, in India and elsewhere. The parallel shift in priorities in scientific research, with stress upon concentration on pressing local problems of production, along with an enormous effort to diffuse the beginnings of a scientific consciousness and some idea of controlled experiment among the mass of the people, deals with a problem well recognized but not so thoroughly dealt with in other countries.

Perhaps the most dramatic developments, however, have been in education. Since the Cultural Revolution, there has been a long and vigorous debate in China over educational policy, the general result of which has been to put power over education at the local level (and most notably in the primary schools) in the hands of committees (boards of governors) composed predominantly of the 'poor and lower-middle peasants'. They determine, with the advice of Party cadres and professional teachers, what shall be studied. They also determine which pupils go on to higher education. The basis of choice is the student's 'political standpoint', which means in the last analysis that he can be trusted, at the conclusion of his education, to come back and serve in the village.

The main aim, in fact, of the present educational system in China is to create a new class of peasant and working-class intellectuals to replace those of middle-class, urban origin on whom China has hitherto depended, and to prevent the dominance among graduates of those who, with the advantage of coming from literate homes (which means essentially middle-class homes), at equal intelligence do better than those from the homes of illiterate peasants.

The problem of preventing the rural areas from being starved of educated leadership is one common to all under-developed peasant countries. The problem of providing real equality of education, when those from intellectual homes have a virtually hereditary advantage over those who do not, is universal. In China it is a severer problem in as much as the children of the poor come not simply from homes with less education but very often from homes with none.

There is more, however, to Maoist educational policy than this; it explicitly aims at the prevention of the emergence of a class of educated technicians and administrators cut off from the working masses. It is worth recalling that within three years of the Russian Revolution, the first complaints were being made of the appearance of a privileged élite; Bukharin in 1923 was already writing about this problem, and insisting that only 'the continuous re-creation of a working-class intelligentsia' would prevent a new stratification of Russian society, which has since to a large extent taken place. In China, with its tradition of domination by an educated élite, the problem is far more acute, and leads to vastly more bitter reactions than in the West.

But we in the West also have this problem of the perpetual tendency of those more socially powerful to perpetuate their advantages by organizing élite schools in which their children form a relatively small group of future rulers and managers whose association in school and college assists them in furthering their careers. What is perhaps of more significance is that our state education system does little to give the mass of the population any sense that their opinions will ever be of much value, or their judgments of any great importance; we do not prepare our population to expect responsibility, and then we complain when they are irresponsible.

Mao's insistence on bending the education system beyond the point of formal equality of opportunity, and in giving positive institutional advantages to those who suffer from social disadvantages, has its parallels in recent American policy towards educationally deprived minorities, and even a parallel in recent proposals in Britain to put the weight of our educational resources not into the teaching of the most successful students (who need least teaching) but into the teaching of average or below average pupils.

The aspect of Maoist education which has been treated with most suspicion in the West is the 'work-study' idea. Schools are encouraged—are in deed under pressure—to permit pupils to spend a part of their time in productive work. The significance of this has been over-estimated. When, in the Cultural Revolution, the students of Peking's agricultural college demanded the right to engage in practical farming, what they sought was *one month per annum only*, working in agriculture. British students of agriculture spend at least three months a year on the farm. The work-study movement was more a reaction to the extreme bookishness of Chinese education than an extravagant movement away from normal educational practice.

There is, of course, an economic side to this policy. Farm children everywhere are expected to work as well as study, except where farming has become so capital intensive that their labour is no longer useful. In peasant societies, the labour of children, at least in the busy seasons, is important: work-study is, among other things, a compromise with farming parents. It also serves, however, to gear education closely to the task of creating a farming population not only familiar with modern possibilities, but able to apply them.

One can illustrate the relevance of Maoism to other poor countries by comparison with developments in India, the only major country in the world which is trying to break out of the poverty trap within the framework of a free Western democratic system. The comparison is forced upon us by India's recent successes in agriculture through the sowing of new strains of grain giving potentially far greater production. This, along with some improvement in other crops, may have raised the rate of increase of agricultural production from 3% per annum to approaching 5% per annum. But this very success may create more problems than it solves. The new strains of wheat demand an effective system of irrigation. They demand higher inputs of fertilizer. They involve considerably more labour at the peak periods of agricultural activity, and so have encouraged the spread of mechanized farming. Only the landlords and the richer farmers have the means or the credit to exploit the new 'miracle wheat'. The poor majority of farmers cannot. The employment of agricultural labourers is cut down by mechanization. The regions with developed systems of irrigation thrive while the rest stagnate. The lack of employment opportunities alternative to agriculture in the countryside forces the unemployed and the under-employed to migrate to the cities in the faint hope of employment there. The problems involved are precisely those which Mao Tsetung has attempted to deal with in China.

Those who find in India's 'green revolution' a democratic alternative to China's 'red revolution' argue that if India's total agricultural production can be increased substantially on the basis of this rich peasant economy, then the benefits will eventually trickle down to the majority, and that India's parliamentary institutions should ensure the necessary redistribution of wealth to the rest of the population. However, all the signs are that this new minority class of capitalist farmers are rapidly joining the other conservative elements in Indian society and are daily gaining in political strength; and it would be optimistic to suppose that the poor peasant majority, illiterate, scattered, cowed, impoverished, and trapped in the caste system, will prove capable in the foreseeable future of taking care of their own interests by effective political organization within the parliamentary system. Perhaps India could learn, in some limited respects at least, from those of Mao's policies which have been developed to deal with similar problems in China.

The relevance of Maoism to the problem of other Communist countries is equally obvious. In a situation in which since 1956 the leaders of the countries of the Communist world have been seeking, though within the cramping confines of their own Stalinist inheritance, an alternative to Stalinist political leadership, Maoism is exerting an increasing influence. There is widespread acceptance that the worst failure of European Communist government has been its reluctance to permit any effective degree of popular participation in the making of decisions and the working out of policy. There is as yet no sign, however, except in Yugoslavia, that participation means more than a reluctant concession by Communist bureaucrats to the need to give more information to their citizens and to encourage them, by intensified exhoration of a kind already only too familiar, to accept the opinions of their betters. Effective participation, however, must mean critical participation. The right to criticize means little unless it includes the right to put forward alternatives. The right to put forward alternatives means little without the right to organize support for alternatives. In committing themselves to belief in the need for participation, these leaders, by the logic of politics, are committing themselves to a degree of freedom far greater than anything of which they are now aware. It is a gulf from which they have drawn back every time they have approached it, where they have not been dragged back by Russian intervention.

The relevance of Maoism to this situation is clear. Although at present the Sino-Soviet conflict has induced most of the Communist governments of Eastern Europe to condemn Chinese thought and practice as un-Marxist, if and when relations between China and the Soviet Union become less embittered, Communist leaders may be able to point to the Chinese model as a means of providing a real though still limited degree of participating democracy within a framework controlled by the Party, a means made acceptable by the Marxist-Leninist terms in which in China this model is expressed and operated.

In Advanced Countries

The final question to be asked is whether the thought of Mao Tse-tung has any relevance to the problems of advanced countries enjoying democratic parliamentary government. Few people in the West would advocate the replacement of parliamentary government by any form of dictatorship of the proletariat, and at our prosperous levels of life (which are partly the consequence of our democratic political system) we do not suffer from social tensions sufficiently serious to make revolution politically possible. It should not be forgotten in the course of our attempts to do full justice to the positive aspects of the theory and practice of Maoism that Maoism also includes features abhorrent to Western liberal values. On every occasion on which Maoist mass-line methods have been fully put into practice, dissenting minorities have been under more severe attack, the independence of the Chinese courts has been destroyed, and judicial procedures have been replaced by politically directed drumhead justice.

The Maoist system is avowedly a dictatorship—the dictatorship of the proletariat, which in China represents only 10% of the population. It is emphatically totalitarian—politics are in command of all aspects of life, to the extent that not even family life is free of political pressures. It is explicitly repressive—dissent, although seldom handled with great harshness and regarded primarily as a problem for education, is permitted only within limits laid down by the revolutionary leadership.

It will not do, however, to separate the totalitarian and the democratic aspects of the Chinese political system into so many *pros* to set against so many *cons,* to be weighted according to the taste and fancy of the observer. The *pros* and *cons* are different sides of an unrelenting attempt to

84

reconcile the necessity for a total war on poverty with the demand for greater individual freedom and dignity. Within the limits to freedom which Mao feels obliged to set, in order to prevent the minority from cramping the development of the poor majority, Maoism enshrines the hope that forced-pace economic growth and individual freedom need not be mutually antagonistic, but that this war on poverty can be so organized that the individual worker or peasant can find in it a greater degree of self-fulfilment than he found in a stagnant society, however individualistic; and that this prospect of self-fulfilment through co-operation with one's fellows can actually become one of the driving forces of material improvement.

This faith is not without its interest to democrats even in countries where mass poverty is no longer a problem. It has become obvious recently in Britain, Western Europe, America, and Japan, that discontent with our political system has increased sharply. Distaste for bureaucratic decision-making, alarm at the influence which our experts exercise over our political representatives, the alienation of our workers by para-military industrial management, concern that our attempts to provide real and effective equality of opportunity have only partly succeeded, anxiety over the shaping of scientific and medical priorities, all these issues in our own society were among the issues which figured in the protests of the Red Guards in China. Radical solutions have been provided in China since the Cultural Revolution, after intense and fascinating public debates and much experiment. The history of these solutions has already been described. It is probable that few of them could be applied unchanged in our Western social and political context.

But the thought of Mao Tse-tung, if it has relevance for us, has relevance of a different order. It is the force and consistency with which he has pursued and expressed certain elements of democracy that makes his thought of universal significance. These elements do not represent the whole of democracy, but they represent those criteria of democratic society which our parliamentary form of government has so far been least able to attain. No democrat can read Mao and be unchanged, though he may reject Maoism as a whole. In this sense, Mao is a classic author whose work represents a permanent contribution to democratic theory.

READING LIST

STUDIES

Li Chien-nung, trans. J. Ingalls & Teng Ssu-yu, *The Political History of China, 1840–1928* (Stanford University Press).

Stuart Schram, *Mao Tse-tung* (Penguin, London).

Stuart Schram, *The Political Thought of Mao Tse-tung* (Praeger).

Jerome Ch'en, *Mao Tse-tung and the Chinese Revolution* (Oxford University Press).

J. Gray & P. Cavendish, *Chinese Communism in Crisis: Mao Tse-tung and the Cultural Revolution* (Praeger).

J. Gray, ed. *Modern China's Search for a Political Form* (Oxford University Press).

Franz Schurmann, *Ideology and Organization in China* (University of California Press).

John W. Lewis, *Leadership in Communist China* (Cornell University Press).

James R. Townsend, *Political Participation in Communist China* (University of California Press).

J. Gray, *Mao Tse-tung in Power: Theory and Practice Since 1949* (forthcoming).

C. Riskin & F. Schurmann, *New Perspectives on China* (forthcoming).

Benjamin I. Schwartz, *Chinese Communism and the Rise of Mao* (Harper Torchbooks, New York & London).

THE WRITINGS OF MAO

The *Selected Works* cover the period 1926 to 1949, in four volumes; the English translation is published by the Foreign Languages Press, Peking, and is available in Britain. Left-wing bookstores have English editions of his main speeches and writings, both before and after 1949. The "little red book" (*Quotations from Chairman Mao*) is obtainable from the same places, and although it is composed of single sentences and paragraphs from a wide range of his writings, it is important as a synthesis of his views on the eve of the Cultural Revolution, intended for popular consumption. Jerome Ch'en has collected other writings in his *Mao Papers*. The only complete collection of Mao's output is at present being published in nine volumes in Japanese; nothing so complete is available in English.